Waiting for Lewis and Clark

Ruth Tuthill Hawes
Endowed Humanities
Fund for History

THE LIBRARY FOUNDATION

Serving the People of Multnomah County

Waiting for

Lewis and Clark

*The Bicentennial
and the Changing West*

David Sarasohn

Oregon Historical Society Press
Portland

Visit our website at www.ohs.org.

Printed in Canada

Distributed by the University of Washington Press

COVER DESIGN: Laura Shaw
INTEROR DESIGN: Veronica Seyd
PRINTER: Friesens, Altona, Manitoba

COVER: Columbia River, Spring 2004

∞ The paper in this publication meets the minimum requirements of the
American National Standard for Information Sciences—Permanence of Paper for
Printed Library Materials, ANSI Z39.48-192.

Library of Congress Cataloging-in-Publication Data
Sarasohn, David.
  Waiting for Lewis and Clark : the bicentennial and the changing West
/ David Sarasohn.
    p. cm.
  Includes bibliographical references and index.
  ISBN 0-87595-295-X (pbk. : alk. paper)
1. Lewis and Clark Expedition (1804-1806)--Centennial celebrations,
etc. 2. Lewis and Clark National Historic Trail. 3. West (U.S.)--
Discovery and exploration. 4. Indians of North America--West (U.S.)
I. Title.
  F592.7.S12445 2005
  917.8--dc22

                        2005019140

Contents

Acknowledgments   ix

Introduction The Trail that Never Ends   3
    Profile / Gerard Baker   10

Chapter 1 Setting Out   17
    Profile / Robert Archibald   31

Chapter 2 The Tribal Trail   39
    Profile / Roberta "Bobbie" Conner   61

Chapter 3 Returning to the Land   69
    Profile / Mary Kiesau   87

Chapter 4 The River Runs Through It   95
    Profile / Maya Lin   116

Chapter 5 The New West, with Postcards   123
    Profile / James Ronda   140

Chapter 6 Legacy and Souvenirs   147

Note on Photographs   173
Note on Sources   175
Index   177
About the Author   182

Acknowledgments

Several institutions helped enormously with this project, and they all deserve their own keelboat's worth of thanks.

In 2002, the Sigma Delta Chi Foundation of the Society of Professional Journalists awarded me the Pulliam Fellowship for Editorial Writers, which allowed me to go out onto the trail and into many Bicentennial Council meetings. Besides this book, the effort even produced some editorials.

The Oregonian, my employer, has been graciously supportive in this effort, especially my boss, Bob Caldwell. The book also benefited from the pointed inquiries of Pat Harrison, who edited the newspaper pieces that were the spines of several chapters here.

The Oregon Historical Society has been crucial throughout the effort, from Executive Director John Pierce's question about whether I had thought about writing a book to Press Director Marianne Keddington-Lang's patient prodding and only occasionally incredulous questioning.

The characters of this book, the people putting together the bicentennial, were invariably helpful and tolerant of questions both ill-informed and repetitive.

My wife Lisa and my son Peter ventured out on parts of the trail with me, and my son Alex was there for us on our return. He was also there when the hot-water heater blew in Portland while the rest of us were deep in North Dakota.

Through the experience, they saw some amazing things and met some remarkable people.

So did I.

Waiting for Lewis and Clark

Introduction

The Trail that Never Ends

Every day, visitors to the Oregon state capitol are welcomed by Meriwether Lewis and William Clark. At the main entrance from the capitol mall, there the explorers are, in heroic mural form, meeting the Indians at Celilo Falls in 1805—and these days, meeting anyone who has business with Oregon.

Lewis and Clark also greet Montanans in their state capitol, in an even more massive mural depiction. In statue form, they welcome visitors to the Missouri state house in Jefferson City. Two hundred years after their moment, Lewis and Clark are still a presence and a guiding force across a huge swath of America—which is more than you could claim for, say, Aaron Burr.

On this winter morning in 2005, the welcome Lewis and Clark extend at Oregon's capitol is particularly expansive. The state legislature is in special session to mark the expedition's bicentennial, and the gathering in the state House chamber—where "Meriwether Lewis," "William Clark," and "Sacajawea" are among the historic names carved on the walls—features the leadership of the state paying tribute to the occasion. The session shows just how closely Lewis and Clark, and their bicentennial, connect to the modern West—development-minded and diversity-conscious—that begins just outside the capitol doors.

Chanting and drumming for the processional and the benediction for the event are provided by the Confederated Tribes of Grand Ronde, tribes who were forcibly resettled in the mid-19th century to the Oregon coastal range from different homelands—including those traversed by the Lewis and Clark Trail. As *The Oregonian* reported in 2004, the Grand Ronde's casino, Spirit Mountain, had just replaced Multnomah Falls as the state's largest tourist attraction. The tribe now claims a role as a major Oregon political player and, in the manner of new power brokers, is also reclaiming its past.

After the processional, both Grand Ronde tribal elder Kathryn Harrison and Oregon Governor Ted Kulongoski called for maintaining Oregon's natural gifts, the natural world depicted in the journals of the Lewis and Clark expedition. Both Harrison and Kulongoski expressed the state's interest in the new levels of tourism expected from the three-year commemoration—especially after major events began in the Northwest later that year.

"We're ready to preserve our natural heritage. The Oregon Lewis and Clark saw will be protected for future generations," pledged the governor, adding, "We're open for tourism. Oregon is ready for its close-up."

For years, similar language and hopes had echoed along the length of the trail, up the Columbia Plateau and over the Rockies, across the plains and down the Missouri to St. Louis—as well as in Louisville, Monticello, and Washington, D.C. What was striking about that morning in the Oregon state capitol—no matter how often and in how many places a listener had heard the call—was the level of anticipation.

People all across the country saw the Lewis and Clark bicentennial as a ripe opportunity, coming at a time when the West explored by the Corps of Discovery was being transformed once again. At a moment of historic change in the region, the bicentennial embodied key elements reshaping its future. From Beltway lobbyists to Northwest Coast tribes and tourism strategists, the bicentennial offered a chance to turn legends into leverage.

Two hundred years after the expedition traversed the territory, people all across the West were waiting for Lewis and Clark.

The Lewis and Clark bicentennial always had a different feel than the nation's own bicentennial, 30 years before. The 200th anniversary of the Declaration of Independence was largely a self-congratulatory event. It reassured Americans, after Watergate and Vietnam, that we were still the people descended from George Washington and Thomas Jefferson. That bicentennial wasn't about what Americans were doing; 1976 was a year-long exaltation of who Americans already were.

But the Lewis and Clark bicentennial, like the original Corps of Discovery expedition, has been about what might happen afterward. The opportunity rose from the confluence of two rich streams—the power of the story and the power of the moment.

Across America, Lewis and Clark have given their names to counties, colleges, cities, parks, wildlife areas, saloons, elementary schools (from Charlottesville, Virginia, to St. Helens, Oregon), middle schools (including one in Tulsa, Oklahoma, hundreds of miles off the trail), taverns, interpretive centers, community centers, real-estate agencies (selling houses as far afield as Massachusetts and North Carolina), car dealerships, a world's fair, a pest-control company, bed-and-breakfasts, churches, tour boat rides, rivers, bridges, bird species, restaurants (including two new ones in Portland just in 2004), and wilderness areas.

Remembering their names has not been a problem.

But in the years leading up to the bicentennial, Lewis and Clark gained new life and power, like an ancient icon that suddenly started bleeding.

The historian Stephen Ambrose's huge national best-seller, *Undaunted Courage*, retold the story of Lewis and Clark as an epic tale of mythic (and Jeffersonian) heroism and judgment, a national saga of connection to the land and to the tribes who lived along the route. The book galvanized readers' interest in the expedition, sending Americans deeper into the literature and out onto the trail itself—where every gift shop sells several different editions of *Undaunted Courage* and locals and leaders recount their own adventures and experiences with Ambrose himself.

Until his death in 2002, Ambrose was a major voice and presence in bicentennial planning, especially in stressing environmental themes. He urged the National Council of the Lewis & Clark Bicentennial to make conservation a major theme and, sitting on the board of the group American Rivers, led it in creating a huge bicentennial project, "Protecting the Rivers of Lewis and Clark." Along with the book and his children, Ambrose's presence persists in a videotaped interview included in American Rivers' traveling bicentennial exhibit, *Discovering the Rivers of Lewis and Clark.*

Similar themes emerged from the expedition's other mass-media boost, Ken Burns' four-hour documentary, *Lewis and Clark: The Journey of the Corps of Discovery.* Over two nights on PBS—and seemingly endless Pledge Week reappearances—the film emphasized the land and the Corps' connection to it, and it vividly connected viewers to what did and did not remain. "Ken Burns spent a lot of time," said John Logan Allen, the geographic authority on the expedition, "and got pictures of the right place at the right time of year."

And as anybody selling a homes-of-the-stars map in Beverly Hills knows, people will go out to look at what they've seen on television.

As the West moves into the 21st century, the timeliness of the Lewis and Clark story springs equally from the nature of the journey and from a new moment that gives it new meaning. More than at any time in the previous two centuries, Americans in 2005 are open to explorers who wrote hundreds of thousands of words on the natural world they discovered and whose relations with the Indians were, as the Ad Council spot on the expedition put it, "notable for the battles it didn't fight."

An age finds the heroes it needs—and the bicentennial that is most useful. Throughout the West, people saw the opportunity in this one.

During the 1990s, the Bicentennial Council and its executive director, Michelle Bussard, worked to stress the tribal role in the Lewis and Clark story and to assemble the Circle of Tribal Advisors, beginning with fewer than a dozen representatives of tribes along the trail. The National Park Service named Gerard Baker, a Mandan-Hidatsa from North Dakota, as supervisor of the Lewis and Clark Trail, and Baker developed Corps II, a traveling exhibit and public forum space to follow the bicentennial across the country.

Slowly, under Baker's urging and encouragement, more and more tribes began to see Corps II as a long-awaited chance to tell their stories—at a moment when the rest of America might actually be ready to listen. Tribal members brought to the bicentennial a powerful frustration of having had other people speak for them. As Baker's brother Frederick told a Lewis and Clark session at Monticello, a tribal joke is that an Indian nuclear family consists of the parents, the kids, the grandparents, and an anthropologist.

The immediate tribal responses to a bicentennial invitation ranged from disinterest to anger. Gradually, some tribes—many with their voices somewhat magnified by casino revenue—began to consider the bicentennial as a way to advance claims of their own place in the West. Tribes that hadn't been too thrilled to see Lewis and Clark the first time—and were still bleeding from the events that followed the expedition—began to look at the bicentennial not just as a painful reminder but also as a tourism and economic development opportunity. By 2005, membership in COTA was approaching 60.

Already, environmentalists—from Stephen Ambrose and national lobbyists inside the Beltway to state strategists drinking around a campfire in Idaho's Bitterroot Mountains—saw a path to their own goals by way of Lewis and Clark's careful depictions of lands and rivers. American Rivers focused on the two massive river systems at the core of the expedition—the Missouri and the Columbia-Snake—both now turned into dammed and hyper-managed chains of lakes, both at the center of political and environmental battles.

The Sierra Club launched the largest campaign in its history, "In the Footsteps of Lewis and Clark," covering a vast stretch and involving thousands of volunteers. The club calculated that national heroes who were also admirers of the land not only could be a conversation starter but—among many westerners not normally given to hugging trees—also a conversation changer.

Besides, those westerners had their own concerns, living in a region that was changing around them. Discovering regional reinvention has been a great American pastime; Americans have talked about a New West as regularly as they have discovered a New South. But at the end of the 20th century, the regional metamorphosis of the West was profound.

Until now, as the trapper and trader West gave way to the homestead West and then to the rancher, miner, and logger West, the resource basis endured, producing an economy that Lewis and Clark might not have recognized but would have understood. But lately, the resource core has widely withered, leaving empty mills and canneries and some even more dramatic effects. Journalists Jack Coffman and George Anthan, studying the Northern Plains on a fellowship, reported in 2004: "It's ironic that as the nation celebrates the bicentennial of the Lewis and Clark expedition, much of the region they opened to European-American settlement is being abandoned." In 1930, the three core states of the Northern Plains—North Dakota, South Dakota, and Nebraska—had 12 members of the House of Representatives; in 2000, they had 5. With the decline of family farms and ranching, the Plains counted some of the poorest—and demographically oldest—counties in the nation.

With the sinking of their historic economic identities, places all over the West, including those along the Lewis and Clark Trail—from the Ohio River through the Plains to the mouth of the Columbia—are looking for opportunities to market their histories. Heritage tourism is the fastest-growing part of the travel business, and the bicentennial seemed a perfect opportunity for trail towns to get more exposure and maybe a moccasined foothold in tourism. In a changing western economy, governors, tourism promoters, and bed-and-breakfast proprietors sought to catch their own ride on the Lewis and Clark keelboat, and Oregon wasn't the only place ready—and eager—for its close-up.

After 9/11, the prospect of massive herds of tourists tracing the routes laid out in the journals faded. But heritage tourism still built steadily, if more slowly than had been hoped, along much of the trail. Unexpected places congratulated themselves on repositioning their images. You had to admire local tourism authorities who spent a good deal of time planning strategies to be at the center of the Lewis and Clark action from now until the tercentennial.

Like so many rivers of the West, the three streams of strategy often ran into each other. Tribes developed their own heritage tourism hopes and devised joint plans with local governments—although not without resentments. Environmentalists argued that tourism and recreation plans depended on preserving natural attractions that people would want to travel to see. And two years into the commemoration, tribes and environmentalists were designing shared TV spots, having identified common interests even beyond the buffalo.

What is truly striking and significant about the Lewis and Clark bicentennial is this new corps of explorers, trying to reach not the Pacific but the future. Unlike the prospects of the original Corps, arrival at this destination is inevitable. But in contrast to even the boldest hopes of Lewis and Clark, these modern voyagers think they can change their destination before they arrive there.

At the beginning of the 21st century, someone seeking the future of the West might be most interested not in Lewis and Clark but in the people interested in Lewis and Clark. Those bringing their own agendas to the bicentennial share something with the first Corps and with the 200 years of the West in between—a powerful sense of expectation, hope, and possibility.

With their anticipation of the potential impact of the bicentennial, they—and much of region around them—were waiting for Lewis and Clark.

Profile

Gerard Baker

Gerard Baker sits in front of a small ranch house on the edge of the Fort Berthold Reservation in North Dakota, a mile of dirt road away from an already lonely stretch of blacktop. Nobody's ever going to say Baker's forgotten where he comes from. He's sitting there now.

He walks up to the road at night these days, he says, and sees three or four lights in the distance. When he grew up here, nights were all black.

Since the 1950s, a lot of things look different.

For three crucial years, Gerard Baker—Mandan-Hidatsa and descendent of the Corps of Discovery's first tribal hosts—was National Park Service superintendent of the Lewis and Clark Historic Trail, the federal bureaucrat holding together the Lewis and Clark bicentennial.

"I'm very proud," said Baker while he was directing the operation, "that the federal effort on Lewis and Clark is being run by an Indian."

The first time around, the tribes weren't as much in control of the situation.

Gerard Baker stands six and a half feet high—plus another couple of inches from his flat-brimmed park ranger hat—often in cowboy boots and wearing a big belt buckle. His face is framed by two long braids wrapped in deerskin he tanned himself in the traditional manner, using the deer's brains. "Every animal," he says, "has enough brain to tan his own hide"—a thought that can give an untanned brain a workout.

"Some people can walk into a room and not be noticed," says Amy Mossett, a Mandan-Hidatsa from North Dakota and the first chair of the bicentennial's Circle of Tribal Advisors. "Gerard Baker cannot walk into a room and not be noticed. He's larger than life. If he was 100 percent Norwegian, it would probably be the same. It's just him."

It was a useful attribute for Baker in the years he spent on an assignment that was larger than likely. As superintendent of the trail, he developed and ran Corps II, a traveling exhibition designed to follow the Lewis and Clark expedition's path over three and a half years. Traveling on two tractor-trailers, Corps II includes two tents—one housing a large exhibit tracing the expedition and the other called the Tent of Many Voices—a portable auditorium where locals, especially Indians, are invited to come in and speak about Lewis and Clark and the history since.

In 2002, the bicentennial's original organizational structure collapsed over financial issues. For several key months, Baker's Corps II was the only solid bicentennial element in place, the core that other programs were built around. He was also the focus of much of the federal funding that seemed the only certain expenditure. He was superintendent of the Lewis and Clark Historic Trail at a time when all trails led to the trail.

In charge of the Tent of Many Voices, Baker was the bicentennial's point man in dealing with dozens of tribes—at a time when many of them, at least initially, wanted nothing to do with Lewis and Clark. Repeatedly, initial inquiries to tribes were met with indifference, or loud resentment. Otis Half Moon, a Nez Perce who worked for Baker as tribal coordinator, recalled contacting a Sioux official and, at the end of a long, angry telephone conversation, being blamed for the Sioux losing the Black Hills. One Standing Rock Sioux called Baker "a government spy with braids."

Baker's attitude, he recalled afterward, was "Get it off your chest and we can talk business."

Before becoming superintendent of the Lewis and Clark Historic Trail, Baker spent more than two decades in the National Park Service, including a stint as the first Indian superintendent of the Little Bighorn Battlefield National Monument. (By the time he left, he had accumulated seven death threats.) In June 2004, he became superintendent at Mount Rushmore—among the Park Service's most high-profile positions, in more ways than one. Of the two other Indians who were Park Service superintendents at the time, one was his son Page Baker, at Arizona's Casa Grande monument.

Long before the assembling of Corps II, Baker had become a widely known figure on the Plains and in the West, a presence who kept erupting into the books of writers trying to make sense of a daunting space and a more daunting history. Dayton Duncan, author of books on Lewis and Clark and collaborator with filmmaker Ken Burns, wrote about trying to gain a feeling of Dakota authenticity by spending a winter night in a Mandan earth hut with Baker—who arranged Duncan in buffalo robes before pulling out a high-tech polar sleeping bag for himself.

In *Great Plains*, an impressionistic account of lighting out for the territory, Ian Frazier wrote about encountering Baker when he was a park ranger at Fort Union on the North Dakota-Montana state line. Baker described the surrounding territory and its history while the two of them fooled around with a double-bladed throwing axe. Then Baker talked of Hidatsa platform burials out in the woods, and Frazier asked excitedly if someone could go out and find one and scoop up beads and pipes.

"Behind his brown eye, a shutter dropped," remembered Frazier. " 'Well,' Gerard Baker said, 'I suppose you could. . . . ' "

When Gerard Baker grew up on the reservation, on the ranch that could see no other lights at night, his parents told him he would have to live in two worlds. When he set out to talk with the tribes as the trail superintendent, Baker repeatedly had to cross between the two, from the federal offices in Washington, D.C., and Omaha to reservations all along the trail—plus reservations well off the trail, in Oklahoma and Kansas, where tribes that had once met Lewis and Clark along the Ohio and Missouri Rivers had been forcibly removed to land the government had figured white people would never want.

The problems came from all sides. The federal government never came up with anything like the $30 million originally proposed for the project. And while a few tribes—notably his own Mandan-Hidatsa—saw an opportunity in the bicentennial, others were variously hostile, reluctant, or indecisive. And changes in tribal governments made it hard to lock in commitments.

"Every time I talk to a tribe, it's different people," said Baker. "If I've got to deal with a dozen different people, that's how it is. It's still a struggle, and it's always going to be."

By Monticello, Baker could point to representatives of 35 different tribes at the event. He was pleased at the level of involvement, explaining in the warm-up tent set up on the grounds, "The whole Lewis and Clark bicentennial is about voices."

Throughout the planning process, Baker kept trying to sign on new tribes and putting out fires among those already enlisted.

"We're still in the process of explaining to tribes it's a good thing," Baker said in August 2003. "They still see [the expedition] as the beginning of the end. I just met with tribes in Oklahoma and Kansas. Right now, they're scared about what's going to happen. They're still talking boycott. They can boycott all they want, people are still going to come."

One reason Baker was so effective in talking with the tribes was that he never hid his own feelings about the government's dealings with Indians. He once commented cheerfully to a Lewis and Clark gathering, as a reception was being planned, "If you're going to have wine and beer, we'll bring along some treaties for you to sign."

To historian James Ronda, "Gerard Baker represents in so many ways the involvement with the story."

As the federal public face of the bicentennial, Baker even fielded objections from tribal leaders who were active in the bicentennial operation. The official National Park Service Lewis and Clark map drew three pages of complaints and corrections about tribes and tribal locations left out or mislocated. At the same time, tribal leaders complained, the map included boundaries of states that in 1804 weren't even a gleam in a geographer's eye.

Baker could hold it all together partly because the attitude toward him, especially from Indians, approached reverence. After Baker was quoted at one Circle of Tribal Advisors meeting in Louisville, one member asked whether Baker was speaking for tribal people or the federal government. There was a brief silence, and then another member said flatly, "Gerard always speaks on behalf of tribal people."

As Amy Mossett says, "Gerard was probably the most incredible ambassador when we engaged in this effort to try to bring people into the bicentennial. If you go back to the time when he was starting out, there were so many tribes just incredulous at the idea that they would be involved. He has this calm wisdom about him. He is an incredibly elegant and effective spokesman."

On the history of tribal treatment by the government, no Indian could fling at Baker a resentment he hadn't felt himself. The family ranch Baker grew up on in western North Dakota is on reservation land, but not on the traditional tribal land. When Lewis and Clark met the Mandan and the Hidatsa, the tribes—then separate but related—were hundreds of miles to the east. In the middle of the 20th century, the federal government built Garrison Dam, creating Lake Sakakawea and flooding much of the reservation where his parents grew up. The feds transferred the Mandan, Hidatsa, and Arikara 200 miles up the Missouri, to a new homeland centered on the emptily but accurately named New Town.

Baker's family made the trip west in a wagon, and his father worked for local ranchers as a cowboy while he cleared the thornapple trees from the family's new land. The experience is still vivid in the minds of tribal people old enough to remember it—or be told about it. "My mom can't even talk about it," says Baker. "She cries.

"We farmed that country since the Creator made us. When they moved us, we couldn't farm this country. I have a hard time when I look at that Garrison Dam now. I hate to see people on that damn lake enjoying themselves.

"When we talk about Lewis and Clark in the last 200 years," says the man most responsible for the survival of the Lewis and Clark bicentennial, "that's what we ought to talk about."

One

Setting Out

After crossing a continent and discovering a new world full of unimagined creatures, Lewis and Clark finally arrived at a Columbia River that they found startlingly "crouded" with salmon.

But they never saw a salmon like this one.

It's 13 feet of papier-mâché with someone inside, dancing along the halls of the student union at the University of Virginia, swimming through crowds that have come to Charlottesville to mark the start of the Lewis and Clark bicentennial. Even for a species of legendary determination, this salmon had come a long way from the mouth of the Columbia.

And—like the 130 representatives of Indian tribes, the teenage fife-and-drum corpsmen, and the mountain-man re-enactors looking so authentic that at any moment they might start scratching—the fish was there for a reason.

"The Snake River salmon saved Lewis and Clark from starvation," explains Lee Anne Tryon Beres of Save Our Wild Salmon. Beres isn't actually the person inside the fish, but she does have a clear agenda, insisting: "The bicentennial is really making it clear to people that salmon restoration is a vital issue."

Along thousands of miles of rivers now unrecognizable to the explorers whose names appear constantly along them, through the vast depopulating stretches and hardscrabble Indian reservations of the Great Plains, in hundreds of advocacy and economic development offices, in the calculations of 82 members of the congressional Lewis and Clark Caucus—twice the size of the congressional Black Caucus—this bicentennial struck Beres and thousands of other people as the perfect medium to send a message.

From its very beginning, the bicentennial was determined to be about more than T-shirts.

In a changing region, three years of national attention—and a once-hoped-for 5 or 10 or 30 million visitors to some part of the Lewis and Clark Trail—glittered as an opportunity to reclaim the region's future. Two hundred years after making their way across North America on a route never followed by anyone ever again, and 50 years after being lost in footnote status, Meriwether Lewis and William Clark had become the most popular and powerful image of the American West.

Over four days, the bicentennial kickoff extended through auditoriums, classrooms, and gathering areas of the University of Virginia up to Jefferson's home at Monticello, where the formal opening event was held. The ceremony was on the west porch, where Jefferson spent decades looking toward the sunset and the Blue Ridge Mountains—never getting past them himself, but constantly pondering what was out there and what it could mean. Jefferson, as historian Donald L. Jackson wrote, spent his life living 20 miles from the end of the world.

When the week's weather turned punishing—who knew how much it could snow in Virginia?—bicentennial planners considered moving the event to a local high-school gym. They dropped the idea—not because the weather got any better, but because the Monticello resonance was deeper than the snow. Still, it was cold enough to remind people that Thomas Jefferson used to complain about frost on his bedroom floor on winter mornings.

The speakers—Lewis and Clark experts, tribal spokesmen, government officials—kept pointing out, to knowing nods and applause muffled by heavy gloves, that the weather was nothing like the 40 degrees below zero that the Corps endured at Fort Mandan or the six feet of snow they slogged through crossing the Bitterroot Mountains.

Lewis and Clark were not just being commemorated. Lewis and Clark were present.

The commemoration "provides some leverage for people to feel a sense of ownership," said Ken Burns, maker of the PBS documentary, *Lewis and Clark: The Journey of the Corps of Discovery*, as he milled around a University of Virginia lecture hall after a discussion on the current state of the lands explored by the expedition. In a room still thick with invocations of connections to the land and historical commitment to it, Burns added, "We need this kind of celebration to remind us of what we value most."

Of course, as a look into display rooms just around the salmon's tail demonstrated, the commemoration was also about T-shirts—and ball caps, and historic maps, and historically accurate rifles, and calendars, and Lewis and Clark candles and jams, and canoe trips, and pewter figures, and a Web site full of Corps of Discovery commemorative consumables.

(That was just a sampling: A few months later, at a planning meeting at Great Falls, Montana, booths also offered Lewis and Clark walking sticks, weather-bound travel journals, note cards, sculptures, cookbooks, CDs, playing cards, posters, mugs, videos, pottery, picture frames, leather maps on wooden easels, buffalo jerky, bicycle maps, patches, and several hundred commemorative pins. Visitors could buy everything but a keelboat to carry it all away.)

As a lever to open up the 21st-century West, Lewis and Clark are particularly sharp and powerful. Their names cover the territory, and over the previous decade Ambrose and Burns—in defiance of calendar realities—gave the captains a head start on their bicentennial. But beyond the influence of best-seller lists or even public television, the path for Lewis and Clark's return was laid by dramatic changes in the nature of the West and the way Americans thought about it.

The Corps of Discovery's 200th anniversary came at the right time.

"This is one of those moments of redefinition that we go through constantly in the West," says James Ronda, professor of western history at the University of Tulsa and a Lewis and Clark oracle—booked solid for the next three years until the 2006 commemoration of the expedition's return to St. Louis. Ronda is speaking at the University of Virginia guest house, sitting in front of an early 19th-century map that depicts the geography of Lewis and Clark's time: states along the Atlantic, territories up to the Mississippi, speculation beyond it.

With the expedition as a powerful symbol in a time of regional transformation, "it's very predictable that groups interested in Western projects should use Lewis and Clark as a vehicle."

For most of the two centuries since the expedition, Lewis and Clark were solid, statuesque, western historical standbys, but not exactly Wild Bill Hickok. "Lewis and Clark were not, during the nineteenth century, the kind of frontier heroes that America favored; they were not like Davy Crockett or Paul Bunyan or Mike Fink or Kit Carson," wrote geographer John Logan Allen. "They were, perhaps, too workaday in their competence, in their matter-of-factness, in their simple approach to doing their job."

From Wild West shows to pulp novels to TV Westerns, flashy figures such as Wyatt Earp and Buffalo Bill were higher-profile heroes, and the theme of the frontier saga was still the rifle and cavalry pistol winning the West.

In the popular culture surrounding the Wild West, real frontier heroism required not a sextant but a six-gun. In the saga of the West, a tree's only role was to be cut down for a log cabin or to provide a hiding place to shoot Indians.

Even at the Lewis and Clark centennial, in 1904-1906, most of the attention went to the captains' Lemhi Shoshone fellow traveler Sacagawea (or Sacajawea, as the Lemhi Shoshone call her), who was made into a suffragette heroine—and the subject of more statues, many of them pointing vaguely toward the horizon, than any other woman in America.

But in the last part of the 20th century, the worldview on the West started to change. Sacagawea still had her fans, but explorers who had carefully catalogued the natural world around them, and who had described tribes instead of decimating them, started to look more appealing to more environmentally minded and diversity-conscious Americans—even off college campuses.

Enter Lewis and Clark and a million words of journals.

The Monticello event directly commemorated a different document, a letter Jefferson had written 200 years ago that day, a letter to Congress suggesting that the United States should send an expedition out past the Mississippi into land it did not own and had at the time no immediate prospect of acquiring. Jefferson estimated it could be done for about $2,500.

The cost overrun would end up at around 1,400 percent.

The president would write several letters about the expedition; and, as historian of science Bob Moore noted at Monticello, Jefferson wrote about different things to different readers. The letter to Congress talked about trade, "extending the external commerce of the United States," a prospectus for an investment. Later, Jefferson's letters to scholars at the University of Pennsylvania and the American Philosophical Society—conveniently, Jefferson was president at the same time of both the American Philosophical Society and the United States—portrayed Lewis as heading off on a research trip, on what could be characterized as a pre-Guggenheim fellowship.

In what may be the third president's most famous letter, instructing Lewis before the trip, he mentioned commerce as well. But he also talked about the lands and the people to be encountered in ways that were then unknown to centuries of exploration. Gaining knowledge of the Indians, Jefferson instructed, was vital: "You will therefore endeavor to make yourself acquainted, as far as a diligent pursuit of your journey shall admit, with the names of the nations and their numbers. . . . Their language, traditions, monuments; their ordinary occupations in agriculture, fishing, hunting, war, arts, and the implements for these; their food, clothing, and domestic accommodations. . . ."

Lewis was also instructed to study things that would greatly interest advocacy groups that wouldn't exist for another 150 years: "The soil and face of the country, its growth and vegetable productions; especially those not of the United States. The animals of the country generally, and especially those not known in the United States; The remains and accounts of any which may be deemed rare or extinct. . . ."

The different attitudes—one viewing the West as a treasure to be mined and carried east, the other seeing the region as a bounty of new people and places to see and know—have clashed ever since.

"The current conflict in and over the West," wrote Montana politician and scholar Daniel Kemmis, "the West that Jefferson took such pains to acquire and explore—might be seen as another Jeffersonian headache . . . arising from deep contradiction and taking decades, even centuries, to work their way toward resolution."

The Lewis and Clark bicentennial, with its themes of stewardship and tribal involvement, is part of the West's working toward resolution. But the captains' 200-year-old interest in the creatures and plants around them—as opposed to other explorers' emphasis on more inorganic material—and their effort to understand rather than eliminate Indians aren't the only sources of their modern appeal.

Besides what they did, there is also who they were.

Writer Dayton Duncan, Ken Burns' collaborator, mused on a Virginia discussion panel that the Corps of Discovery reminded him a bit of the original *Star Trek*—a moody captain and a diverse crew. (He also noted that a few years earlier, gatherings of Lewis and Clark buffs could also remind you of *Star Trek* conventions.)

The Corps of Discovery, after all, looks a bit like a post-modern version of the old World War II movie platoons. Instead of a southerner, a farm boy, an Irish-American, and a private from Brooklyn, the Lewis and Clark story had a roster of 21st-century diversity: the leaders of dozens of tribes, Clark's African-American slave York, and of course Sacagawea—a teenager who was also a working mother.

So while the ceremony from the west porch of Monticello in 2003 included the requisite politicians, Lewis and Clark buffs, and proud local boosters, the program also included many more Indians—and in different roles—than the celebrators of the Lewis and Clark centennial might ever have imagined.

Speaking to 2,000 people and two centuries, Daniel Red Elk Gear of Virginia's Monacan tribe had a question: "People say they traveled through hostile tribes. If they made it through, how hostile were we?"

The Monacans, from the Monticello area, were not previously considered a trail tribe, and their presence reflected an expanded view of the Lewis and Clark Indian community—and for the western tribes, a different view of the eastern tribes.

Karenne Wood, a Monacan poet, led off with a poem for the occasion, reminding the audience:

"Nothing was discovered.
Everything was already loved."

To some in Indian Country, the whole idea of tribal participation in the bicentennial has been controversial. "There should be no reason the Indian nations of this region should celebrate the anniversary of the Lewis and Clark expedition," wrote Tim Giago, a South Dakota Oglala Lakota editor and columnist. Those who would join in, he thundered, were "grabbing on and riding the coattails of an expedition that only brought them destruction."

The bicentennial's planners had their own worries, reflecting the 1992 quincentennial of Columbus' voyage, an event that turned into an ethnic crossfire and a public-relations disaster.

At the University of Virginia in Charlottesville, only a few miles from Monticello, a panel discussion with eight tribal representatives ran long, jutting into the next event on the schedule. It seemed as though Indians, actually getting a chance to talk, had a lot they wanted to say. One questioner identified himself as "of the Blackfeet nation in the place you people call Montana." The phrase reminded listeners—although some didn't need reminding—that the only two Indians directly killed by the expedition were Blackfeet.

In the West, as Faulkner said about the South, the past isn't dead; it isn't even past.

"We first had to convince tribes all along the trail that we were not celebrating Lewis and Clark, but it's a huge story," said Amy Mossett, a frequent public portrayer of Sacagawea—or Sakakawea, which means Bird Woman in Hidatsa—and a tourism director for North Dakota's Mandan, Hidatsa, and Arikara Nation. Mossett was one of the earliest Indian voices in the bicentennial.

"When I think about our effort, it's not really about Lewis and Clark; it's about who we are," she explained.

The opportunity to explain that to a wider audience—the University of Virginia lecture hall was full, and C-Span was taping—seemed to galvanize the occasion. Sam Penny of Idaho's Nez Perce seized the moment to deliver an eight-part history of Indian-white relations. For many, the subject seemed more personal.

"When I was 18, I left. I didn't want to be Indian any more. I worked on oil rigs and joined the military," said Darrell Martin of Montana's Gros Ventre tribe. "I came home. I found it doesn't matter where you go, you're still who you are."

The gathering had the sound of people who had decided who they were.

"I have watched my elders endure horrible things," said Bobbie Conner of Oregon's Confederated Tribes of the Umatilla Indians and vice president of the National Council of the Lewis & Clark Bicentennial. "But they have been gracious and polite, because we know something that those who insult us do not: We're going to be here forever."

Throughout the halls of the University of Virginia and the sitting rooms and grounds of Monticello were the tribal representatives, in bright colors and decorated robes amid the tweeds of the academics, the carefully re-created uniforms of the re-enactors, and the khakis and winter outerwear of the tourists.

"Everybody realizes Monticello would have been a dud without the tribes," said Barbara Allen, Oregon's bicentennial coordinator, a few months later, "not just because of the pretty feathers—although that was important—but because of the vision."

The presence and the respect were already a change, and Karenne Wood later praised the kickoff as "a truly multicultural event"—not exactly a common compliment. Still, Bobbie Conner later recalled a Monticello problem, painful to the tribes but maybe less immediately clear to others: too little thought given to how tribal elders, revered as both authority in the present and connection to the past, would manage in a hilly and unexpectedly frigid situation. It was, she later explained, humiliating.

The trail still has a ways to go.

But just as the bicentennial rests on a changing view of the people on the land before Lewis and Clark's arrival, it also hangs on a different view of the land itself.

"Lewis and Clark weren't very interesting to Americans in the 19th century, when they had more wilderness than they knew what to do with," said Robert Archibald of the Missouri Historical Society, president of the Bicentennial Council. "Now, Lewis and Clark are a barometer. We can look at the West through the eyes of their journals and get a sense of what we've lost."

The environmental history of the West is bound by two lists. On one end are the hundreds of species first described by Lewis and Clark; on the other are the western creatures on endangered or threatened species lists. Several, such as grizzlies and some kinds of salmon, appear on both.

In 2002, a Sierra Club survey found that of 122 creatures first presented in print in the journals, 49 were at some level of government concern, from threatened to extinct. "We could consider the justifications for the conservation of endangered species," wrote environmental historian Daniel Botkin, "in terms of many of the species first described by Lewis and Clark."

The Corps of Discovery seems both a connection and a lifeline.

Around the corner in the University of Virginia student union, the Sierra Club promoted its campaign to protect the lands explored by Lewis and Clark. Starting years ago, the group churned out vast arrays of material on preservable spaces along the trail, including a call——printed in Lakota—for saving the Black Hills: "Tokatakiya Unci Makoce Tiwahe Icata Awanyan: Protect Grandmother Earth for our Families, for our Future."

In a more familiar medium, the Sierra Club also unveiled a new 45-minute movie about protecting the trail, narrated by Sissy Spacek. The organization promised to blaze a bold new trail of conservation, and, pledged Executive Director Carl Pope, "Lewis and Clark will be our guides in this journey as well."

Pope and the Sierra Club had another guide as well. A decade earlier, it had occurred to Dr. John Osborn, a Spokane-area environmental activist and newsletter publisher, that the bicentennial would be a terrific opportunity for environmental advocacy. Within a few years, Osborn was portraying William Clark at the National Press Club in Washington, D.C.

Osborn is an internist, specializing in AIDS and working at the Spokane Veterans Administration hospital. Advocacy is a second full-time career. Asked how he manages it, he looked as if he didn't quite understand the question, and said it was just a matter of getting up at five in the morning—and of being married to an attorney who specializes in water law and Indian law and shares his priorities.

"I'm kind of at peace with myself. I've done all that I can do to make sure conservation will be a theme of this," Osborn explains in the University of Virginia student food court, talking about the land and the Columbia River. "The monument that the nation needs to build to commemorate Lewis and Clark is a free-flowing river."

That idea is shared by American Rivers, whose own bicentennial project can't even fit into the University of Virginia. It's laid out on a basketball court in a shopping-mall health club about two miles north of the campus—big displays of photos, text, and charts chronicling the Missouri's evolution from a river to a shipping canal. Looming out of all the maps and pictures is a giant photograph of a North Dakota Indian, in suit and tie, bursting into uncontrollable weeping at the decision to build a dam that would flood his land.

For many visitors, the photo and the event would be the strongest memory of the exhibit. Other visitors could remember the event without the photo.

The exhibit was designed to travel the country, part of the largest effort in the history of American Rivers. The campaign emerged in the late 1990s, urged on by two national figures who then died too quickly—CBS commentator Charles Kuralt and historian Stephen Ambrose.

"The Missouri River could be as much of an economic engine for tourism as the Rocky Mountains and the oceans are to those states," argued Rebecca Wodder, president of American Rivers. "What the bicentennial brings to us is a stage to tell the story of what the rivers were like 200 years ago, and what we can do now."

In the next three years, the exhibit would be seen by more than a million people, who saw its call for recreating a Missouri River that Lewis and Clark could recognize. That ultimate goal was about as likely as seeing Thomas Jefferson saddle up at Monticello and ride toward Washington, D.C., but the group would settle for trying to help the Missouri—and the Columbia and the Snake—become rivers that looked more like rivers.

And American Rivers thought it saw a chance.

The group even had one heartening example. The fourth river in its Lewis and Clark project, Montana's Yellowstone—navigated by Clark on his way back east—is the longest free-flowing river in the United States.

Back at the university, surrounded by a dozen people in maroon North Dakota Tourism shirts, Governor John Hoeven seemed ready to put the expedition up for the winter all over again. Hoeven's constituency could be the poster state of a changing, and sometimes waning, West. North Dakota is the only state with a smaller population in 2004 than it had in 1930—those residents who remain have pondered changing the state's name to the less polar-sounding "Dakota"—and the bicentennial seems a way to give a shout out to the world.

Tourism has just passed energy as North Dakota's second-largest business, Hoeven said, and history-based tourism "is the number one growing experience in terms of what people want. That's a fit for us. That's what people are looking for, especially in the urban areas."

Hoeven also has an interest in other bicentennial themes and has just discussed them with one of the event's key speakers. "We need to re-think the way we manage the Missouri River," he says firmly, "and protect fish and wildlife in the upper reaches."

North Dakota is sponsoring the biggest state tourism promotion at the Monticello event. But upstairs at the University of Virginia student union, states from Virginia and West Virginia to Washington and Oregon are also pushing their Lewis and Clark sites, with receptions and pins and enough media kits to swamp a canoe. Lewis and Clark interpretive centers are the newest cash crop, and states that find themselves counting less on wheat and timber are intensifying their drive to harvest more travelers' checks.

"If we're successful," says Clint Blackwood, who heads Montana's bicentennial effort, "we'd like Montana to be known as the Lewis and Clark state for the next hundred years." His state is banking heavily on a lot of tourists, and it's not as if it has many alternatives.

"Several years ago, there was a sense that rural Montana could hunker down and wait it out," Blackwood says. "Now, small ranchers and farmers get bought out. People who want to weather the storm are in for a long wait."

So Montana is launching Lewis and Clark-evoking programs such as "Undaunted Stewardship," encouraging ranchers to maintain and open up trails and helping farmers diversify into bed-and-breakfasts. At the far end of the trail from Monticello, southwest Washington has invested heavily in new roads, a path along the beach with Lewis and Clark sculptures and mementos, and an active campaign to remind people that Washington state was where the Corps of Discovery reached the ocean. Oregon was just where it happened to spend the winter.

"Tourism is about the third most important industry in the United States," notes geographer John Logan Allen. "It doesn't take a clever politician to figure this out, and politicians are figuring this out. Every trail state has built, or is planning, a Lewis and Clark Trail center, hoping to draw visitors not only during the bicentennial but for a long time to come."

At Charlottesville, 11 states and the federal government released a market survey showing rising interest in trail tourism, with bicentennial awareness tripling. Tourist promoters—from state-underwritten operations such as North Dakota's Fort Mandan to individual entrepreneurs such as Idaho's Barbara and Harlan Opdahl, who run horse tourism trips—reported rising interest.

On this icy weekend, Charlottesville was full of people seeking to seize the moment. The West is changing, and three years of national attention—and a stream of heritage tourists—glittered as an opportunity to claim the region's future.

The Lewis and Clark centennial, a hundred years and a different world ago, was marked by world's fairs at both ends of the trail—in St. Louis in 1904 and in Portland in 1905-1906. We don't do world's fairs any more. They lose money and, besides, too many Americans have now traveled the world to make it a thrill for the world to come to us. More important, it may be that the unbounded enthusiasm for technology that drove U.S. world's fairs, from Philadelphia in 1876 to New York in 1964-1965—and certainly St. Louis and Portland—doesn't run quite so strongly these days.

We've come to see the advance of civilization as more complicated than simply accepting new devices, from electric lights at the Chicago Columbian Exposition of 1893 to television at the 1939-1940 New York World's Fair. Historian Mark Spence has suggested that the themes of the Lewis and Clark bicentennial—tribal involvement and land stewardship—are exactly the reverse of the themes of the 1904-1906 centennial, which hailed the triumph of white American civilization and technology over uncooperative tribes and territory.

The Portland world's fair in 1905-1906—the Lewis and Clark Centennial and American Pacific Exposition and Oriental Fair—was marked by the world's largest log cabin, exhibits from 21 countries and 16 states, and rides on two motorized blimps. Like the bicentennial, the centennial fair had a significant tribal presence, but the message wasn't quite the same. "The greater part of the exhibit," explained the superintendent of Chemawa, a federal Indian school just north of Salem, Oregon, "is devoted to industrial and literary training given pupils in the Indian schools, and showing their ability to take up the pursuits of our own race."

In 1905, for the America of the Lewis and Clark centennial, the attitude toward tribes was about instruction. This time, it's about listening.

And instead of a major forestry exhibit demonstrating how much of nature we could remodel, this time it's about how we could preserve.

What persists is the enormous iconic power of Lewis and Clark—literally, in America, names to conjure with—to be once again the vehicle for thousands of miles of hopes and plans. As shown by the response to Stephen Ambrose's book and Ken Burns' documentary and the drive by so many states to connect to the bicentennial, considerable numbers of Americans identify with the spectacular journey of a few dozen people who traveled from St. Louis to the Pacific Ocean and back—a group changed by what they saw and ultimately changing everything they encountered.

The Lewis and Clark expedition, James Ronda mused at Monticello, was a voyage into imagination as much as into unexplored land, a trip into "the country of the mind out past St. Louis." The bicentennial covers the same territory, but with a different map and different objectives. The story was then, and still is, says Ronda, "Who we were, who we are, who we might yet become.

"We find what we look for. We uncover what we seek out."

In 1805 or in 2005.

Profile

Robert Archibald

"St. Louis," said Robert Archibald in the tones of someone making a quiet confession, in the late-night voice between privacy and pride, "is the great unexpected love of my life. I care more about St. Louis than any of the rest of it."

And then there was the matter of his $7 million bet.

For seven years, as the bicentennial approached, Archibald, head of the Missouri Historical Society, had assembled the ultimate blockbuster Lewis and Clark exhibition. The museum world these days is largely about blockbuster exhibits, massive traveling collections of Van Goghs or Byzantine artifacts that come with their own gift shop and coffee-table catalogues and raise an institution's profile like a tire jack. Since coming to the Missouri Historical Society from Montana in 1988, Archibald had assembled several major exhibits, including a multi-event tribute to a local son, jazz trumpeter Miles Davis.

The Missouri Historical Society was in a unique situation for Lewis and Clark. It had a substantial collection of its own, since St. Louis was the beginning point of the expedition—and presumably a key focal point of the bicentennial—and Clark had spent the last 30 years of his life in St. Louis as U.S. Indian superintendent and sometime governor of the Missouri Territory. Cataloging and borrowing, the Society assembled a collection of more than 500 items—tools and clothing and books that had either gone on the expedition or gave a sense of life and lore at the beginning of the 19th century. After eight months in St. Louis, the exhibit would go on tour to Philadelphia, Denver, and Portland and then finish at the Smithsonian, carrying the awareness of Lewis and Clark—and of the Missouri Historical Society—back and forth across the nation.

Then, in the summer of 2002, the bicentennial collapsed.

Technically, what collapsed was the organizational structure of the national Bicentennial Council, based at Lewis & Clark College in Portland, which had developed ambitious plans and very little fundraising. The operation had some successes, notably the creation of the Circle of Tribal Advisors, but it could no longer cover the salaries of its staffers. It certainly had nothing like the $2 million needed to cover its new crown jewel. The Ad Council—creators of the advertisement "A mind is a terrible thing to waste" for the United Negro College Fund—had committed to developing a series of bicentennial public service ads worth as much as $168 million.

A 30-second spot is a terrible thing to waste—not to say hundreds and hundreds of spots all across the country.

To Archibald, the bicentennial structure that he had expected to bolster his $7 million project also looked like a terrible thing to waste.

He went back to the Missouri Historical Society board with a proposal: He would become head of the Bicentennial Council, which would operate out of the Society. The Society would become a co-sponsor of the Ad Council effort—putting up $1 million in front money and lending the Bicentennial Council the other $1 million.

It came out to a lot of museum admissions. And it wasn't like Archibald didn't have other things to do.

The Missouri Historical Society is a substantial operation, one of the four big property-tax-supported institutions—along with the art museum, zoo, and science center—that ornament Forest Park in the west of St. Louis. In his 15 years there, coming from graduate school in New Mexico and the state historical society in Montana, Archibald had built a major extension onto the building and expanded its fundraising and membership. He had a weekly spot on local public radio talking about history, was chair of the Cultural Action committee of the local movement St. Louis 2004, and was a leader in an effort to reform the St. Louis city charter. He was writing several books. He had recently been diagnosed with Graves' disease, a form of hyperthyroidism that led him into a grueling stretch of steroid treatments.

And at the time Archibald faced the collapse of the Bicentennial Council, he was also running for public office. He was part of a four-member ticket, including a former mayor, seeking—and likely—to take over the St. Louis school board.

Still, he went to the MHS board, proposing that it part with a great deal of his time—and a lot of money. They bought it.

Were they happy about it?

"It would be to everyone's advantage for us to take the lead," recalled the board's chairman, W. Wayne Withers, a top executive at Emerson Electric. (The new wing of MHS is the Emerson Center.) "'Happy' was not the word."

Still, says Withers, the board saw an opportunity.

"It's very unusual for a state and local operation to go national, but we felt it was a great opportunity. Obviously, it was publicity for St. Louis from a national perspective."

For why that seemed so important, it is necessary to turn from Archibald, and even from the Missouri Historical Society, and look at St. Louis.

In the 2000 census, St. Louis—a founding member of the National League, the city at the junction of the nation's two greatest rivers— had a population of 348,149, placing it right between Colorado Springs and Wichita. Yet, St. Louis has the cultural resources of a much larger city, because it once was.

At the time of the Lewis and Clark centennial, in 1904, St. Louis was the fourth largest city in the United States, much bigger than anything west or south of it, with the largest railroad station in the world. Since then, the city's rank and population have dropped. Just since 1990, its population has dropped 12.2 percent, the highest rate of population loss among the top 100 U.S. cities. Its signature monument is the Gateway Arch of the Jefferson National Expansion Memorial, a tribute to the westward movement, and the favorite local joke is that St. Louis is the only city that built its monument to the people who left.

"One of the things that the Lewis and Clark bicentennial does for St. Louis is to give us something to feel good about," Archibald explained a few months after taking over. "I'd like that city to celebrate. It does well enough at commiseration."

To Wayne Withers, taking over the bicentennial "was almost a form of civic duty, which may sound a bit corny in this day and age."

And so, in the summer of 2002, the Missouri Historical Society signed on, and Archibald announced publicly: "St. Louis was at the center of things in 1804, it was again at the center in 1904, and now it will be at the center in 2004. Hurrah for St. Louis!"

And if other spots along the trail murmured when out of 15 Signature Events 4 of them were awarded to the St. Louis metropolitan area, it wasn't their institution on the line.

"A year and a half ago, I had a bankrupt organization on my hands," Archibald remembered about the takeover. "I said, I'm going to give this three months, and if I can't put this back together, we'll have to declare bankruptcy. It's like I bet everything on being able to pull it out."

Archibald quickly discovered, as the previous management had, that no major corporation seemed eager to throw in several million to identify the Lewis and Clark bicentennial with Coke or Federal Express. (There might have been a problem with a slogan, "When it absolutely, positively has to be there in two and a half years.") But he did raise $3 million from Emerson and $500,000 from local brewer Anheuser-Busch for the Society's own exhibit. He faced disagreement on the council between tribal voices and Lewis and Clark traditionalists and walked the tightrope policy (and his own impulse) of carrying a stewardship message without toppling into a political agenda.

He managed to hold it together. With his big head, square face, and floppy brown hair, Archibald somewhat resembles a compressed Garrison Keillor and operates with a similar style of low-key bursts of eloquence and persuasion. After years of maneuvering through the political and corporate worlds of St. Louis, he brought to the bicentennial a shrewd sense of organizational possibilities and power arrangements. "Bob is a very good chairman," commented David Nicandri, the head of both Washington state's bicentennial effort and the Washington State Historical Society. "He knows when to let things go, and when to cut them off."

Then the bicentennial was awarded a $2.5 million grant from the Hewlett Foundation, which eased pressures considerably. A year after Archibald took the gamble, he could say, "I can see my way through it. I can see how the bicentennial comes off. I can see how the debts get paid. I was losing sleep over this 10 months ago. We've come a long way."

By then, Archibald had been elected to the school board and had gone through a baptism considerably hotter than fire. School board meetings exploded in 2003 when the new majority moved to maintain a full school year by closing some local schools and laying off the system's janitors. One of the other three board members placed a public curse on the new members and the mayor. Archibald found himself eating dinner at midnight after evening meetings that just kept going.

By the end of 2004, the school board faced the prospect of a strike, and at one meeting members were given bags of coal as Christmas presents. Archibald told the *St. Louis Post-Dispatch* that constant attack on board members' character and motives gave the job "a real personal cost."

Still, he insisted, the board was the right place to be.

"If historians are serious about their discipline, they're obliged to be civically engaged," Archibald argued. "Why spend your time evaluating the decisions human beings have made in the past, and not enter the fray?"

The school board immersed Archibald in the race-pervaded politics of St. Louis, themes that arose on virtually every board decision and every city battle. The issue also came up, less bitterly, on the bicentennial front. Recent accounts of the Lewis and Clark expedition, from a contemporary perspective, have put more emphasis on Clark's slave York—notably on Stephen Ambrose's point that the discussion on where to fix the 1805-1806 winter campground made York the first slave in American history ever to vote. The bicentennial produced books on York, and Louisville set a statue of him on its riverfront near where Lewis and Clark met to begin their trip. Archibald hoped York would help spur "significant African-American involvement" in the bicentennial events.

But the idea never seemed to intrigue large numbers of African Americans. Possibly it was harder to see York, a slave with no choice about going on the expedition and with no reward after its completion, as their idea of a heroic model. Deep into bicentennial planning, Archibald had another idea: "I want to get the president to do an emancipation proclamation for York. If we can make Clark a captain, we can make York free."

He might have hoped for White House access, since Laura Bush had agreed to become honorary chair of the bicentennial—although nothing much seemed to come of it.

The traveling Lewis and Clark exhibit spent eight months at the Missouri Historical Society in 2004, and, to Archibald, "The exhibit has been an absolute blockbuster." Visitors to the exhibit were actually fewer than projected, 146,000 rather than the 175,000 to 200,000 expected, but Missouri Historical Society membership nearly doubled, and the institution's profile zoomed, with coverage in major national newspapers, the BBC, *Le Monde*, and *The Economist*. To Archibald, it made the Missouri Historical Society "a regional museum that suddenly has catapulted into national and international status," and, as he told the *Post-Dispatch*, "People were aware of what we were doing and it reflected well on St. Louis."

That fall, he accepted the 2004 St. Louis Award, given to the "resident of metropolitan St. Louis who, during the preceding year, has contributed the most outstanding service for its development."

St. Louis might be the unexpected love of Archibald's life, but at least it's not unrequited.

Still, his effort to overhaul the St. Louis city charter was overwhelmed at the polls. "We got trounced, for a variety of reasons," he said a few months later. "I'm trying to be philosophical about it, even though I spent $3 million of other people's money."

By the following spring, Archibald was calling a new meeting of the reform forces to decide whether to try again. He was setting off on two new books. He was beginning the process of assembling another Missouri Historical Society blockbuster exhibit on the Revolutionary hero George Rogers Clark, William's older brother—who was, Archibald notes, a much bigger American icon during the 19th century than Lewis and Clark.

One afternoon in 2003, well before the opening of the Lewis and Clark exhibit, Archibald slipped from his office to the Society's library a few fields away across Forest Park. White-gloved librarians brought out an expedition journal bound in elkskin. Archibald circled the book, looking at an artifact at the core of his collection as if he had never seen it before.

"This is why I'm in this business," he said softly, in non-public figure tones. "It's not just something in a history text. It really happened. Look at that," he demanded, pointing to an illustration as precise as if executed in a studio instead of a wilderness. "These guys aren't amateurs."

And it's always good to work with a professional.

Two

The Tribal Trail

It was just the kind of new relationship that the Lewis and Clark bicentennial was supposed to create, in just the place where 200 years ago it all started.

In July 2002, President George W. Bush kicked off the bicentennial in the East Room of the White House, with a call for a wider understanding of all of the peoples involved. Tribal people whose ancestors had encountered the expedition two centuries before were heavily represented, including the Chinook from southwest Washington, who had recently gained federal recognition as a tribe and had brought the president a gift of a dugout canoe. Addressing the group, Bush said of Sacagawea, "Her courage and her strength remind us that American Indians have played a central role in our history, and their unique culture must never be lost."

Two days later, the Department of the Interior stripped federal recognition from the Chinook. The tribe's leaders then declared that they saw no point in participating in the bicentennial at all.

During the next few years the Chinook would reconsider—several times.

Over more than a decade, tribal involvement in the Lewis and Clark bicentennial has been a lot like the original expedition itself. It has often been halting, uncertain of its direction, and marked by misunderstandings and language barriers. For some groups, such as the Chinook, the process has been as disappointing as the discovery that there was no water route to the Pacific. But, like the expedition, at the end tribal involvement came a very long way.

In the 1905-1906 Lewis and Clark Exposition in Portland, Indians were a picturesque afterthought, to be uplifted like the United States' more recently conquered Filipinos. But in planning for the bicentennial, years before the first re-enacting boat dipped into the Missouri, tribal involvement was declared the first theme of the event. It was decided very early, for perhaps the first time in a major national event, that the occasion would not be celebrated.

It would be "commemorated"—because so many of the people most involved didn't see much to celebrate.

The first statement encountered on the bicentennial's Web site urges visitors to see "why the National Council encourages reference to the bicentennial as a commemoration, not a celebration."

Yet, as the process and planning went on, as dozens of tribes became involved—and a few dropped out—as the bicentennial dealt with tribes that had been forcibly removed from the places where they met Lewis and Clark and with tribes decimated by disease and disaster, a new theme began to emerge.

Slowly, many tribes began to see the bicentennial not just as an awkward imposition but as an opportunity—a chance for economic development, for tourism, and for developing a market for tribal arts and handicrafts—as a moment to connect to mainstream economic and political leadership. But most important, from the Ohio Valley to the Pacific, there was a chance for tribes to tell their story, to explain that Indians were not just, as the expedition's journals often declared, "pore and dirty."

The public legend of Lewis and Clark, tribes and historians say, is only half the story. There are also unconsulted oral histories of the expedition, a view not just from the rivers where the expedition traveled but also, as James Ronda says, from the banks where the tribes watched.

There are, according to an old writers' adage, only two plots in the world: Someone goes on a trip, and a stranger comes to town. The Lewis and Clark story has legendarily been the first; the bicentennial declares that it is also the second.

And while the bicentennial is careful with the language of commemoration and not celebration, another theme peeps up from the planning.

"One of the things that I have told tribes along the trail is that we do have something to celebrate during this bicentennial," says Amy Mossett, an enrolled member of North Dakota's Mandan-Hidatsa and a bicentennial planner.

"We can celebrate the fact that we survived Lewis and Clark. And everything that happened after Lewis and Clark, we survived it all."

The distance between the East Room of the White House and the gritty Sioux reservations of South Dakota is vaster than anything Lewis and Clark could cover. The nine reservations spread across the state are centers of poverty, early death, and unemployment, with the jobless rate at Pine Ridge—located in the Badlands of the state's southwest corner—approaching 80 percent.

At Pine Ridge, when the residents think western history, they don't think Lewis and Clark. They think Wounded Knee.

Understandably, the South Dakota Sioux—who, it should be said, weren't very pleased to see the Corps of Discovery the first time around—produced some of the bitterest opposition to tribal participation in the bicentennial, from the writer Tim Giago to Alex White Plume, who led a band of protestors to disrupt bicentennial events in the state in the fall of 2004. The Standing Rock Sioux, who live along the North Dakota-South Dakota state line, participated in events but were what you might call unenthusiastic about remembering Lewis and Clark.

"They didn't do anything," objected LaDonna Braveheart, the Standing Rock Reservation's tourism manager. "They came up the river on a little boat. They had no knowledge of the country. To us, they were like these people wandering around the wilderness lost."

The Lewis and Clark bicentennial was not exactly a longtime dream of Daphne Richards-Cook either. When the idea came up, the head of the state's Alliance of Tribal Tourism Advocates recalls, "I wanted nothing to do with Lewis and Clark. Right now, when I read the journals, I get mad."

The journals, after all, described the Sioux as the "vilest miscreants of a savage race."

But at the urging of the state's tourism director, Richards-Cook, then promoting tourism for the Lower Brule Sioux Reservation in the middle of the state, put together a fast PowerPoint presentation on the possibilities of Sioux involvement in the bicentennial. The next thing the University of South Dakota graduate knew, she was coordinating a national Signature Event.

Still, her ideas on the explorers may be a little different from the ideas of some other folks on the national Bicentennial Council.

"We can use it not to honor them," she says firmly, "but to market us."

Tribal reservations on the Great Plains have grim aspects, with stretches of bad road and aging trailers. But the land itself can be stunning, rolling off in tans and browns and greens—the Lower Brule

Reservation has some very successful agricultural operations—toward a horizon somewhere just short of the Rockies.

A year before the bicentennial entered her territory, Richards-Cook talked about it in the middle of the Lower Brule Reservation center, a few blocks from a small, distinctly unglitzy but moderately lucrative casino. That weekend, the reservation marked its summer powwow, a cross-cultural burst of dancing and chanting; dazzling if not entirely authentic costumes trimmed with mirrors, shells, and beads; temporary burger and Indian Taco booths; kids shooting Silly String and teenagers wearing NBA jerseys; and hours of careful and competitive dancing.

Within just a few blocks, the center's paved streets peter off into gravel, and the few suburban-style homes are quickly replaced by bare-bones single-wides. The reservation's unemployment rate, she says, hovers around 40 percent.

"When Lewis and Clark came, we were rich," she says. "We had the fur trade, we were rich in language, in culture, and in common ownership of the land. We controlled most of the Great Plains. "

The impact of white settlers on the Dakotas leaves many Sioux dubious about hosting any more arrivals, even as Richards-Cook tries to present it to the tribe as a business proposition.

"I've gotten resistance here. People don't understand," she says. "We need to leverage resources again, but in a different way, like leveraging horses changed everything before"—in the 18th century, when mastering the new Spanish stallions gave the Sioux control of the Great Plains.

In Richards-Cook's living room on the Lower Brule—she's since moved to Rapid City, in the western part of the state—was a stunning ceremonial robe, part of a dazzling Sioux art collection. Inside, her sons played on their video game set.

Not everyone in the tribe could balance two worlds that way.

Still, she made it clear, not everything would be for sale. Tourists wouldn't be offered Sun Dances, sweat-lodge experiences, or tours of sacred sites. Sacred sites are an explosive issue all over Indian Country, where there is a fear that a wave of white tourists might disrupt the sites even if they didn't want to—and nobody is confident they wouldn't want to.

Still, it's an opportunity in places where there haven't been many. The tribes, and Richards-Cook, planned to offer different tourism packages, from crafts to cuisine and nights in a Plains tepee—which, despite impressions from *Peter Pan,* is about the same size as a Manhattan studio apartment.

Tepees sit in front of a lot of Dakota homes, like tool sheds or playhouses in more populated areas. These days, a tepee's outside is more likely to be made of synthetic fiber than buffalo or deer hide, but the principle is the same: a fistful of long poles arranged in a cone and a fabric (usually white) wrapped around it—and the endless prairie sky peering in through the hole at the top.

With a sleeping bag and maybe an air mattress, tourists might not be precisely replicating the early 19th-century Plains experience, but it would be a lot closer than staying in a Motel 6.

Lately, South Dakota Sioux have managed some significant success in the wider world. They were vital to the re-election success of Democratic U.S. Senator Tim Johnson in 2002 and to Stephanie Herseth's two victories in 2004 for the state's U.S. House seat. Strong Sioux support couldn't quite re-elect Senate Minority Leader Tom Daschle that year, although he appeared at every powwow on every South Dakota reservation and publicly persuaded Giago to abandon an independent campaign and endorse him.

The question is whether the Sioux can handle tourists as well as politicians. Or as well as they handled horses.

The idea that the Lewis and Clark bicentennial would have a different attitude toward the tribes was established before people knew much else about the occasion. One of the elements driving the late 20th-century popularity of the explorers, after they had spent so many years in the shadows of western heroes with prime-time weekly television series, was that Lewis and Clark were open to dealing with Indians without shooting them—even if that was partly because, in the Corps of Discovery's case, shooting wasn't numerically feasible.

Then, post-1960s scholarship on the expedition revealed the tribes' much larger and more crucial role in the success of the expedition. As bicentennial planner Chet Orloff put it, it wasn't a white guys' camping trip.

Perhaps most crucially, planners got to see the disaster of the Columbus quincentennial in 1992—which collapsed in a blast of angry tribal attacks and charges that honoring Columbus actually celebrated half a millennium of genocide.

From very early on, bicentennial planners wanted the Lewis and Clark event to work differently. Allen Pinkham of Idaho's Nez Perce recalls an argument in the mid-1990s with the Lewis and Clark Trail Heritage Foundation, the national group of Corps buffs, when he insisted that tribes would never celebrate the expedition. "To us," Pinkham said in 1999, "Lewis and Clark certainly aren't heroes."

Led by Executive Director Michelle Bussard, the Bicentennial Council emphasized an Indian role and devised the Circle of Tribal Advisors, or COTA.

"Michelle was very dedicated to maintaining that tribal voice," recalled Bobbie Conner. "She kept us meeting, although many times we thought nobody was listening to our agenda."

By 2001, a meeting in Omaha declared tribal involvement the highest priority of the Bicentennial Council.

COTA emerged around Pinkham and a core of strong-minded women, including Amy Mossett, the group's first head; Bobbie Conner; and Dark Rain Thom of Ohio's Shawnee Nation United Remnant Band. The group functioned even after the fiscal collapse of the bicentennial's original organizational structure.

"When there was a need to do some restructuring, the tribal component was still intact," remembered Mossett. "Those of us on COTA remained working together."

Planning and preparation were vital on things as basic as the National Park Service's Lewis and Clark maps. "It used to make me nuts," said Conner, talking about multiple correction requests sent to NPS, "that the original map had states that didn't exist when Lewis and Clark came and there were no tribes. We need to make a map on which Indians are not poster children but property owners."

At the same time, there were also things that COTA wanted off the maps—such as tribal sacred sites. Too many items that tribes consider sacred have ended up in either the Smithsonian or tourists' living rooms. While tribal involvement was the top priority of the

Bicentennial Council, COTA's top priority was cultural resource protection.

That concern also runs all the way back to Lewis and Clark. According to legend, large parts of the collection of Indian artifacts, carefully assembled and brought back by the expedition, ended up decorating University of Virginia fraternity houses.

Prospects improved when the operation of the council was taken over by the Missouri Historical Society—trying to protect its $7 million investment in its traveling bicentennial exhibit—and improved further when the Hewlett Foundation announced a $2.5 million grant to the council, which produced $1 million for tribal involvement.

As it often does, money created possibilities, and it helped the Bicentennial Council and COTA work together. Now there was a grant program for tribal projects, as well as a program to sell tribally made pouches. A tribal message would be included in the Advertising Council's campaign of public-service radio and TV spots, and COTA would have its own public-service spots—designed by an Indian-owned ad agency.

Of course, as you can hear from anyone who has ever served on a committee—especially any committee about public messages, especially any committee cutting across cultures—opportunities can be complicated.

The contracts for pouches—which ended up selling out fast—went largely to tribes who made early commitments to the bicentennial. Other tribes, and tribespeople, later complained about the arrangements and decisions.

"I come to this conference, and I see the amount of imitation that goes on. Why wasn't tribal liaison put first?" demanded Arlene Adams, of Montana's Salish-Kootenai, at one COTA meeting in Great Falls. She also had a specific complaint about the pouch process: "I don't mean no offense to anybody, but when you want to go back in time, cowhides weren't a part of that time. I've heard from people that different things were submitted, that were authentic, that weren't selected."

One theme idea from the Advertising Council creative people—"The farther from civilization they went, the more civilized they became"—was disliked by some COTA folks, who didn't like the idea that when Lewis and Clark went into tribal lands, they were leaving civilization. They had the same reaction to a line noting that before Lewis and Clark discovered the West, two million people had already discovered it.

"Nuances became important," explained Robert Archibald, president of the Bicentennial Council. "They felt Indians didn't discover the land, they came out of the land."

Even at the end, when council members were looking at finished TV spots, tribal representatives had concerns. Indians featured in the spots, they worried, looked too grim. They would bolster the stereotype of the stoic red man, and what tourist would want to visit people who didn't smile?

But just having the conversation, putting out the TV and radio spots, and emphasizing tribal involvement and cultural protection as key elements in a three-year national commemoration marked a unusual level of white society talking to Indians—and, more important, listening to Indians.

"This is truly," promised Archibald, "one of the potential lasting legacies of the bicentennial."

Forging a tribal role in the Lewis and Clark bicentennial, and building a legacy out of it weren't easy. Some tribes didn't want to participate, and constant changes in tribal councils would set previous agreements back. "We'd see people for two months," remembered Dark Rain Thom, "and then nothing from a tribe for two years."

Many tribes, forcibly transplanted from where they were in Lewis and Clark's time, had to be brought back from their exile to provide tribal involvement for events held in their previous homelands. Tribes disputed heritage rights with other tribes and raised the question of who was and wasn't an Indian. Federally recognized tribes didn't want to share platforms and resources with nonrecognized tribes— and partly due to the burst of tribal dissolution in the 1950s, there are a lot of nonrecognized tribes. And Lewis and Clark buffs invested in the heroic image of the expedition have limits to their tolerance of revisionism.

"I find myself sometimes in the role of cultural mediator," said Archibald soon after taking leadership of the council, "trying to explain that there can be very different views of this, and nobody's lying."

But the arguments start right off with Sacagawea—or Sacajawea, or Sakakawea.

On most of the statues and plaques throughout the West—and she is, by one count, the most depicted woman in American history—she's called Sacajawea or Sacagawea. The story is clearer than the name. She was a Lemhi Shoshone captured as a child by a Mandan raiding party, married young to the French trader Toussaint Charbonneau, and brought with him on the Lewis and Clark expedition, where she gave birth to the son Lewis and Clark called Pompey and, at a crucial point, was reunited with her brother, then a Lemhi chief.

The Lemhi Shoshone proudly claim Sacajawea, who as the bicentennial approached was honored on a new dollar coin—although the model, Randy'L He-dow Teton, was actually not Lemhi Shoshone but Shoshone-Bannock. But Sacagawea is also claimed by the Mandan-Hidatsa, who contend—and who some believe have been winning the argument—that her name is actually Sakakawea, Mandan for "Bird Woman." That's her name on the statue dedicated in October 2003 in Statuary Hall of the U.S. Capitol, representing North Dakota—although it might also have honored her as "the heroine formerly known as Sacajawea."

The two tribal groups have another difference on the subject. While the Mandan-Hidatsa have been deeply involved from the beginning, the Lemhi Shoshone, now about 480 strong and not a federally recognized tribe, have refused to participate in the bicentennial or to join the Circle of Tribal Advisors. The attitude of the tribe—the one Sacagawea was born into, with whom she reunited in one of the expedition's most dramatic and crucial moments—shows the complexity of tribal responses to the bicentennial and how 200 years of history lies over everything like a trade blanket.

The problem, explained Lemhi Shoshone tribal leader Rod Ariwhite, is that the tribe is no longer where Lewis and Clark could find them. In the late 19th century, gold was discovered in their northern Idaho territory, and the tribe was gradually moved 200 miles south as a minority lodger on the reservation of the Shoshone-Bannock.

Before joining the bicentennial commemoration, the Lemhi Shoshone want to go home—or at least start the process.

"The ties my people have to that valley are hard to explain," says Ariwhite. "That's why we were called the salmon-eating people. That valley created our identity. We came from the mountains, and lived there 10,000 to 12,000 years."

No tribe, insists Ariwhite, contributed more to the success of the expedition—which included not only Sacagawea but her half-Lemhi son Pompey.

"They asked for a guide. All we're asking for is the same kind of assistance," says Ariwhite. "Lemhi country is still 96 percent federal land. The last thing we want to do is uproot anybody. We know what that feels like."

Ariwhite explains this as he drives a truck through the hills of New Mexico, where he is director of operations for the Pueblo Laguna reservation—he commutes from Idaho. He's actually a longtime student of Lewis and Clark. While he won't join the formal bicentennial process, he has participated in some events honoring Clark, for whom the tribe feels a particular closeness—partly, maybe, because Clark educated Pompey in St. Louis.

The bicentennial, says Ariwhite, has stirred some support for the Lemhi Shoshone's claim. But Dan Whiting, spokesman for Idaho's powerful senior senator, Larry Craig, says the issue has been around for a while and doesn't seem to be getting much closer to a resolution in the tribe's favor.

"They need to be a recognized tribe first," says Whiting. "That would be the first step, before they apply for a new reservation. We don't have a short-term plan to introduce legislation on this."

Still, Ariwhite sees a possibility—and an opening. If Lewis and Clark reappeared, he argues, "They would like to come back and see the Lemhi prospering."

Early on, the Bicentennial Council set the core principle that any Signature Event needed tribal co-sponsorship. It wasn't always an easy principle to maintain. In 2003, one state official complained that some states were having trouble achieving tribal involvement. Amy Mossett responded that after years of activity by COTA, "I find it disconcerting that someone is having trouble finding tribal participants for their events."

At early bicentennial events, complained Bobbie Conner, "tribes were not thanked, not introduced, not given thank-you gifts. Local officials were thanked, but not the tribes."

The Hewlett grant made things easier, but problems deeper than thank-you notes remained. For the early Signature Events that followed quickly after Monticello—in Louisville, southern Illinois, St. Louis—the tribes who greeted Lewis and Clark are now long gone from the scene, shipped west by treaties and troops. To provide tribal participation, descendants were invited back to their old territory as tourists.

In 1803, the Shawnee were the largest tribe in the territory that would later become Indiana, across from Louisville, Kentucky, where Lewis and Clark met to begin their trip down the Ohio. For the bicentennial event commemorating the moment, the Shawnee were designated the major participating tribe.

But which Shawnee?

By 1803, the Shawnee had already been pushed west from native territory in Pennsylvania. By 2003, they had been pushed west twice again, ending up in Oklahoma in three large tribal groups. But the sponsoring tribe back on the Ohio was a group called the Shawnee Nation United Remnant Band, which is not recognized by the federal government—the band's Web site notes that the Shawnee chief Tecumseh never signed a treaty with the United States—but is the only tribe recognized by the state of Ohio. By the bicentennial, it had fewer than a thousand members, on a standard of at least one-sixteenth Shawnee descent, and had bought several small parcels of land.

"We're buying Ohio back," explained Dark Rain Thom, "one acre at a time."

But the larger Shawnee community, tens of thousands in Oklahoma, had a skeptical view of the United Remnant. Their feeling was, as Gerard Baker, then National Park Service superintendent for the Lewis and Clark Trail, noted, "East Coast Indians are so mixed up with whites, they're making it up as they go along." Louisville would be, he noted, "a delicate situation."

Many western Indians believe there are barely any tribes east of the Mississippi—to which Thom often responds, "Who do they think kept the whites off their backs for 250 years?"

Early encounters were tricky—and the complications were reported by the local press, to considerable tribal resentment. But as the 10-day event in October 2003 proceeded successfully—it drew 100,000 people, well beyond expectations, although in Louisville terms, it was no Kentucky Derby—relations seemed to ease. Finally, at a panel on tribal issues at Locust Grove, the estate of William Clark's sister, Ohio Remnant and Oklahoma remainder got on cordially.

"I wasn't knowing what to expect," the Park Service's Jeff Olson told the *Louisville Courier-Journal*. "To have the Shawnee get together without a hitch was one of our best times over the last nine months" of bicentennial arrangements.

In the St. Louis area, with three 2004 events marking the beginning of the expedition up the Missouri, there was hardly any tribal remnant. The dominant Missouri tribe of Lewis and Clark's time, the Osage, was long gone. In 1808, William Clark, then Indian superintendent for the territory, forced a treaty on the Osage—a people who had never gone to battle against the United States—that ceded virtually the entire state of Missouri for compensation of about 10 cents a square mile. Clark later told a friend, according to biographer Landon Jones, that "it was the hardest treaty on the Indians that he ever made, and if he was damned hereafter, it would be for making that treaty."

But 200 years later, the Osage were willing to return from Oklahoma for the Signature Events, to make what you might call a special guest appearance—partly encouraged by the St. Louis Art Museum that joined the bicentennial by mounting the largest exhibit ever of Osage art.

The Osage reappearance in Missouri went well, leaving behind the prospect of continuing tribal relationships with Missouri institutions and help for Osage language preservation.

"It was a matter of contention," admitted Leonard Maker of the Osage about the original invitation to join the bicentennial. "The tribe did have to consider what our response would be. We can't fight 200 years, but we want to tell our story."

In St. Charles, Missouri, on the May 2004 weekend that marked the bicentennial of the Corps' departure, Maker stood in the Corps II Tent of Many Voices, where he'd just shown a 12-minute movie on Osage history to about 60 people. "We're still here," he told them firmly. "We're not a museum piece. We're a vibrant and living people."

Two hundred years ago, he estimated, about 10,000 Osage lived in the area. Now, after the tribe's long residence in Oklahoma and intermingling with other tribes and settlers, Maker estimates the number of full-blooded Osage in the world at seven—and that he, looking to be in his 50s, is the youngest. He is accompanied by his wife, from another tribe, and his three children, including a daughter wearing a sash reading "Jr. Miss Indian Oklahoma"—and looking like any teenager might in that situation.

Maker himself looked like an urban planner, which is his job for the tribe. He was pleased to be in St. Charles and noted that there hadn't been this much Osage spoken in Missouri in 200 years. Coming back had been worth it, he thought, and the local response had been warm—maybe because in Missouri these days, Osage are exotic.

Just like the original Corps of Discovery, the Lewis and Clark re-enactors were surprised by the Sioux.

Lewis and Clark themselves, at least, were prepared for it. In 1804, the Sioux were seen as the most hostile tribe on the known part of the route, the only one mentioned specifically in Jefferson's instructions to Lewis. The Sioux controlled a stretch of the Missouri in what is now South Dakota, and the expedition did indeed have a near-violent confrontation before it could proceed up the river. In their journals, Lewis and Clark had harsh, derisive words for the Sioux.

In 2004, as the re-enactors appeared in Chamberlain, South Dakota, they were confronted by a group of Sioux led by Alex White Plume of the Pine Ridge Reservation—the recently elected vice president of the Oglala Sioux. White Plume told the re-enactors they were not wanted in Sioux country, that the original expedition had brought only disaster, and that they should stop their journey and go back.

If they didn't, some of the protesters suggested loosely, the Sioux might return with bows and arrows. It was, Amy Mossett recalled, "a pretty intense meeting."

The re-enactors, who had been dealing with official tribal leadership, were taken aback. White Plume, who raises horses and buffalo—

and, he explained, faced major federal charges for raising hemp on his property—declared himself furious both at the re-enactors' coming into South Dakota and at the comments of their leader, a descendent of William Clark.

"I expected an apology," said White Plume a month afterward. "He said, my great-great-grandfather loved you people—and 'you people' is a racial slur. He's trying to gather up our stories, make a mint, and continue to leave us here. We have a beef with this country. We're tired of living in genocide. We're dealing with historic grief and trauma. We're trying to get back to what's natural for us."

What White Plume wanted to talk about was not Lewis and Clark—he thinks events should instead honor Sioux heroes such as Sitting Bull, Crazy Horse, and Young Man Afraid of His Horses—but the Black Hills. The 1868 treaty covering the Black Hills, he says, was a 100-year lease. The century is up, and the Sioux should get the Black Hills back.

As to the potential for economic development, White Plume said that one event where he protested featured the re-enactors, some tribal people, a few bicentennial officials, and "three tourists, who got lost and happened to stumble in. That's their economic development."

The South Dakota Signature Event—Oceti Sakowin, or Seven Council Fires of the Sioux— was planned as a major occasion. It was a month long with events in several locations, the first tribally directed Signature Event. Afterward, Daphne Richards-Cook—by then on the national Bicentennial Council—didn't disagree that, economically, things turned out a little flat.

"We did have people in Chamberlain, 5-10,000, but not the tens of thousands expected," she says. "Maybe it's going to happen down the road, but it didn't happen to us."

The 2004 Signature Events in Nebraska and North Dakota, before and after South Dakota, actually drew more people than expected—not hundreds of thousands, but a solid 50,000, maybe more, in each place. Maybe Oceti Sakowin was too long or too diffuse—or maybe the tribal element, in operation and attraction, was more of a complication than expected.

Or maybe Alex White Plume and his supporters had a point.

"I talked to the protesters," said Richards-Cook. "There's so much hurt and anger in our tribes." And Lewis and Clark are still a touchy point to her, even after she's put two years into their bicentennial: "I don't look at the journals. Every time I get madder."

Richards-Cook was disappointed but not discouraged. "It was quite the experience," she said. "It was a very educational experience." For one thing, it was educational about what it meant to work with groups outside the reservation.

"A lot of times you develop partnerships, and they say they're going to do things for you, and they do," said Richards-Cook, "but they tell you how to do it. It turned into a whole different experience. Next time we do the partnerships with non-natives, it will be our way.

"Non-Indian people have to learn that Indians don't want to be window dressing."

And she thinks the bicentennial has provided connections for the next time, for an expanded Sioux art auction and for different Sioux territory tours that the Alliance of Tribal Tourism Advocates will package and offer itself, giving the tribes' own view of their lands and lives.

"We don't want to be living exhibits," said Richards-Cook. "We don't want that to happen again."

Of all the time when the survival of the Corps of Discovery hung on tribal help, perhaps the most fragile and flickering was the moment when they stumbled out of the Bitterroot Mountains in September 1805, starving and tattered, into the arms of the by-no-means delighted Nez Perce—whose immediate instincts were not entirely hospitable.

"There was a big debate," says Allen Pinkham, former chairman of the tribal executive committee, telling the story from tribal oral tradition. "People said, 'Let's kill them, they're not going to do us any good.' But we knew they possessed things we didn't have," notably guns that the Nez Perce needed against hostile tribes. So the Nez Perce fed and sheltered the collapsing explorers. They then helped Lewis and Clark get to the Snake River, watched their horses over the winter, and guided them back over the Bitterroots the next summer.

Leaving the Nez Perce, Lewis wrote, "These affectionate people our guides betrayed every emotion of unfeigned regret at separating from us."

In the long-term, however, things didn't turn out as the tribe had hoped.

"There have been few better examples of Indian-white relations in the United States, where the Indians have been so consistently friendly and the whites so treacherous," wrote geographer John Logan Allen, "than the long history of Nez Perce and American contacts."

Three-quarters of a century after the Nez Perce saved Lewis and Clark, the U.S. government forced one band of Nez Perce to leave their historic lands in Oregon's Wallowa Valley for a reservation in Idaho, sparking conflict that convinced the band to flee. A group of 750, only a third of them warriors, set off on an evasive and circuitous 1,200-mile effort to reach sanctuary in Montana or Canada, outmaneuvering and sometimes outfighting the U.S. Army before finally being stopped, in the snow, 40 miles short of the Canadian border. The group's leader, Chief Joseph, then reportedly delivered what has become one of the most famous and wrenching speeches in western history, translated and possibly enhanced by Lt. Charles Erskine Scott Wood. Wood's reported account, published almost immediately in *Harper's Weekly*, concludes: "Hear me, my chiefs. I am tired. My heart is sick and sad. From where the sun now stands, I will fight no more forever."

Afterward, the surviving Nez Perce were shipped off to Kansas and then Oklahoma. It took them years to get back to the Northwest.

In Montana and Idaho, the Nez Perce Trail approaches and cuts across the Lewis and Clark Trail, like parallel aisles headed in different historical directions.

Today, the tribe counts a membership of about 3,400, based around the Nez Perce Reservation in the narrow neck of northern Idaho in the Clearwater Mountains—between Lapwai and Kamiah. The area is thick with Lewis and Clark sites, including Weippe Prairie, where a starving Clark first met the Nez Perce in September 1805, and the Long Camp, where the expedition waited in May and June 2006 for the snow to melt before trying to head back over the mountains.

When the bicentennial came up, Gerard Baker remembers the Nez Perce dropping in and out of involvement with the planning. Idaho Senator Larry Craig, talking about the pain and complications of tribal history and how they shaped uncertainty and reluctance about involvement, recalled, "I had to be taught that. The Nez Perce were very insistent."

But Allen Pinkham—descendant of the Lewis and Clark figures Red Bear and Cut Nose, former Forest Service official, former Marine, author, and storyteller—became involved early on with both the Bicentennial Council and COTA, on his own clear terms. Slowly, he remembered, the attitude and openness shifted, to a point where tribal involvement became more realistic.

"If we want to get any kind of benefit out of it, we've got to participate," Pinkham said in early 2005. "We could get irate and throw rocks at canoes as they come down the Clearwater River, but that's not going to get us what we want."

And Pinkham knew exactly what he wanted from it all.

"We want to tell our story, and say we're still here in Nez Perce country," said Pinkham. "My feeling has always been that we've got to go out and kill some myths about Indian people. We're actually doing a lot of things out here people don't realize. People don't realize we're a major player in wildlife restoration."

In early 2005, the tribe was struggling in the Idaho legislature on a water agreement, a debate in which the Nez Perce claimed to speak in defense of the salmon. When the deal was reached, the Idaho government was attacked by some white property owners and the Nez Perce executive committee by some tribal members, both charged with selling out historical rights.

To make its point, the tribe ended up hosting Idaho's only Signature Event, Among the Nimiipu—the tribe's own name before white explorers called them the Nez Perce. The June 2006 event, predicted Nez Perce organizer Bill Smith, would be "the most aggressive of them all. We're going to build some friendship and trust and try to get the word out."

Over more than a decade, the tribe's involvement with the bicentennial has followed a path as circuitous as Chief Joseph's.

"We have to work with all kinds of attitudes," noted Pinkham, after a decade of involvement. "People say, 'You guys are trying to change history.' I say, 'Wait, you guys have left out my history from my perspective.'"

Six months after the Bush administration revoked the Chinook's status as a recognized tribe in July 2002—it was nothing personal, said the Bureau of Indian Affairs spokesman, "but the tribe did not meet the seven criteria established under the law"—they were back making their case at the Lewis and Clark kickoff at Monticello.

"We are still here," Cliff Snider of Portland, honorary chief of the Chinook, declared at the Monticello tribal panel. "Despite displacement and disease, the Chinook are a sovereign tribe. And there are Chinook salmon, Chinook winds, a Chinook army helicopter, the Chinook Winds casino, and Chinook, Washington. If they say we don't exist, that's a misnomer."

The day before, the exuberant 75-year-old Snider spoke at the Tent of Many Voices in one of its first high-profile appearances. He had been told, he said, not to talk about the recognition issue, but it still left him plenty to say, as he recounted his tribe's oral traditions about Lewis and Clark.

"You know," he told three dozen people who may never have seen a Chinook—or heard of one—"how history is."

And how it never quite goes away.

Early in the process, the Chinook were enthusiastic at the prospect of participation. "I think it will create economic and job opportunities for the tribes, too," hopefully suggested tribal leader Gary Johnson. "There's a lot of requests for tribal participation, for selling cultural items, traditional items, baskets. I think the people that come on the Columbia River, following the Lewis and Clark journey, many of them will want to take home some items with them."

Chinook trade with visitors goes way back, well before the Corps of Discovery. In fact, Lewis and Clark found that Northwest Coastal Indians' experience with European and American trading ships made them hard bargainers, to the captains' annoyance.

In the spring of 2005, a replica of the first U.S. ship to visit the region, the *Lady Washington*, visited the coast and was met by two Chinook canoes.

"Globalization started on the Columbia over 200 years ago with northern Europe trade beads intersecting English gun flints, Chinese porcelain, Hawaiian coral and god knows what else at Station Camp,

Fort Vancouver, Fort George," mused Jim Sayce, a planner of the local bicentennial efforts. "20 decades + has brought trade, a new government, new disease, new knowledge, new immigrants, new communities, and yet, there for their grace go the Chinook."

Even after the denial of federal recognition, there was still the hope of using the bicentennial to build support for full tribal status. "The Chinook saved Lewis and Clark's life," argued their congressman, Brian Baird (D-Wash.). "We need to incorporate them for their benefit, and our benefit."

But as November 2005 and the Signature Event on the Northwest Coast approached, the Chinook faced another threat that they considered the ultimate deal-breaker.

Another Indian group, the Clatsop-Nehalem, declared its plan to participate as the representatives of the Clatsop, the tribe that lived south of the mouth of the Columbia in 1805-1806. The managers of the event explained that any tribal group was welcome, but the Chinook—who maintain that they are the rightful descendants of both Chinook and Clatsop—announced that, in that case, they would not be involved.

"They don't deserve equal recognition or equal billing," Johnson told the Vancouver, Washington, *Columbian*. "From our perspective, they don't exist as a tribe. We are the long-standing governmental representative of the historic Clatsop tribe."

The Chinook now total about 2,300 people, including about 500 Clatsop. The Clatsop-Nehalem, depending on estimates, have around 100 members. "We do not want any flak occurring between the Chinook and the Clatsop-Nehalems," declares Joe Scovell, a retired teacher and chairman of the group. "We're claiming our own identity, our own rights, and we don't have anything to do with the Chinook tribe."

In 1851, Scovell notes, the Clatsop had a treaty separate from the Chinook. Since then, argue the Chinook, the two tribes—like many others around the country—have merged.

By the end of 2004, the Chinook declared that they would boycott the Astoria-based Signature Event, Destination: The Pacific. Tribal cultural committee chairman Tony Johnson explained: "The tribe has said it's simply going to reserve the right to be heard in any way we think necessary." The Chinook, he said, might participate in places where the Clatsop-Nehalem were not involved.

Later, the Chinook loosened their position and said they might find ways to take part.

"We went to great lengths and effort to keep them on board," Amy Mossett told *The Oregonian* in November 2004, "but we're not forcing Lewis and Clark on anyone." Cyndi Mudge, director of Destination: The Pacific, said the situation was "like being in the middle of a huge family disruption."

The Chinook have their own tribal oral tradition about Lewis and Clark, and there is an ancestor called Needle Woman, named for her trade with the expedition, buried in their cemetery. The Clatsop-Nehalem have enlisted Dick Basch, a trial liaison officer for the National Park Service, who traces his ancestry to Coboway, the Clatsop chief who traded with Lewis and Clark during their winter on the Oregon coast.

Basch is staying out of the argument but sees reasons why problems keep coming up with tribal involvement.

"The bicentennial is a plus for tribes, an opportunity for disclosure, but it's taxed the tribes," says Basch. "Tribes don't put this as a high priority. Tribes have many other things on their plate, and they just don't have the resources."

Involvement with the bicentennial was an opportunity, but it came with costs—organizational and emotional—that tribes were sometimes unable or reluctant to pay. Even after arrangements were made, strains and disappointments and old grievances would often break out and cast a shadow over bicentennial planning.

For many outsiders, the Chinook's resistance to the Clatsop-Nehalem seems excessive, even petulant. In late 2004, the Vancouver *Columbian* compared the Chinook to "a stubborn teenager who won't be seen with a social rival."

The Chinook position may be overblown, and it may change or be negotiated down. But it does seem there is more to it than a juvenile sulking. To the Chinook, their identity has been challenged by both the federal government and the Clatsop-Nehalem, and maybe there's a reason they consider their identity particularly important.

You could say it's most of what they have left.

Among the dozens of tribes involved in the Lewis and Clark bicentennial, one of the most powerful feelings—aside from general anger about two centuries of mistreatment and objections to being characterized as stoic and humorless—is a resentment that white people have been explaining them and speaking for them. The first thing that Gerard Baker told any tribe was that the Tent of Many Voices would give them the opportunity to speak for themselves, to explain its version of the Lewis and Clark story and to talk about the things that had have happened to the tribe in the 200 years since. No matter how high or how long the anger, tribes found it an intriguing invitation.

"It's the first time," said Daphne Richards-Cook, "we're getting to tell our story."

The full Lewis and Clark bicentennial—from Monticello, down the Ohio, up the Missouri, across the Rockies, and down the Columbia to the Pacific—runs more than 5,000 miles and then thousands of miles back. But from the perspective of dozens of tribes—from the Monacans in Virginia to the Mandan-Hidatsa in North Dakota, the Nez Perce in Idaho, and the Umatilla and the Chinook in Oregon—the trail is much longer.

It runs for more than 200 years. And there is no going back.

Marilyn Hudson, who runs the Mandan-Hidatsa-Arikara museum in New Town, North Dakota—a modest building around the corner from the casino, but one of the few museums anywhere with an original Jefferson Peace Medal carried by Lewis and Clark—wouldn't say that most tribal members are enthralled by the bicentennial. "The average citizen on the reservation," she figures, "is pretty ambivalent."

But, Hudson says firmly, what they do believe is that the past is a beginning and not an end.

"The spirit of America is that it bounces back," she says confidently. "We identify very much with the idea that we're all Americans."

Profile

Roberta "Bobbie" Conner

Bobbie Conner has lived in a lot of places, but she has always known how to measure where she was.

Denver—where she was a high-ranking bureaucrat in the Small Business Administration—was a 20-hour drive from the Confederated Tribes of the Umatilla Indian Reservation, just outside Pendleton, Oregon. Sacramento, her last assignment as one of the nation's 69 SBA district directors, was "eleven hours, any way you go"—up through Portland, or the back way east of the mountains.

Growing up all around the Northwest, as her single mother earned three degrees and followed a teaching career, Conner remembers "always going home. If we weren't going home, they were coming to see us. And every summer we'd be with my mother's extended family on the rez."

Conner represents her own confederation of tribes, being part Umatilla, Cayuse, and Nez Perce. Her grandmother was a niece of the Nez Perce chief Young Joseph, a potent lineage in northeast Oregon. Once, on the subject of politically correct definitions of Native Americans, Conner grinned that her grandmother just called herself a River Indian.

Wherever she was, Conner always knew where she was from. That certainty followed her through years of building the Circle of Tribal Advisors, starting with a handful of tribal members and growing to representatives of dozens—but never all—of the tribes who once lived along the Lewis and Clark Trail.

By the 200th anniversary of the departure of the Corps from St. Charles, Missouri, Conner was vice president of the National Council of the Lewis & Clark Bicentennial and a major figure in shaping the commemoration.

She has been a potent voice both in establishing tribal involvement as the top priority of the bicentennial—"We're not the backdrop," she says, "we're part of the landscape"—and in disputing tribal critics who say that Indians should have nothing to do with marking the beginning of their cataclysm.

But to Conner, as she explained at the January 2003 gathering at Monticello, "We've been a part of the Lewis and Clark commemoration not because it's fun—necessarily—but because we're still here."

That celebration of survival—a flag of identity planted in the middle of a hostile history—explains a lot about what Conner is doing. That "necessarily"—a verbal wink tossed into the middle of a passionate statement of principle, with a kilowatt-level glint in her eye—explains a lot about her.

Bobbie Conner got into the bicentennial by way of history. After graduating high school in Pendleton and then finishing a degree at the University of Oregon, she worked for the United Indians of All Tribes Foundation in Seattle. Then—picking up a Willamette University degree in management along the way—she began a rise in the federal bureaucracy. After she had reached the highest regional levels of the SBA and there seemed no place else to go, Conner got an offer to return to Pendleton to run the Umatillas' new museum and cultural institute, Tamástslikt. Being a shrewd bureaucrat, she first managed to get herself loaned to the museum by the SBA and then, in a few months, became director and a tribal employee.

She knew the institute was where she wanted to be. "One of the reasons our tribal council took a leap of faith and built the institute was to humanize our people," said Conner. "The vision of us has been so dehumanized by Hollywood, through literature and in history books."

At the same time, nobody in or out of Indian Country is faster to see the point where Hollywood—and history—turns into comedy. "Lots of my family members were in B Westerns in the '50s," she explained to a Lewis and Clark gathering in 2003. "We think of them as home movies, and they're fun to watch." In the midst of a firm insistence on the tribes' claim to their own history, Conner can point out deadpan, "We're so fond of old things we collect cars."

The Tamástslikt Cultural Institute, organized around the theme "We Were, We Are, We Will Be," announces to visitors: "We are a small group of people who have maintained our traditional song, dance, art, language, clothing, religion, and food, despite significant events and changes in our lives. We are a small group of people with a big story to tell."

Tamástslikt is just across a driveway from the Umatillas' Wild Horse Resort and Casino, and the buildings reflect the tribes' two survival strategies. Tamástslikt tells the story of tribal history and presence in the Columbia Basin, and—after years of unfilled government promises—the casino profits largely paid for it. Conner doesn't apologize for the gambling boom that has made the Umatillas a leading employer in eastern Oregon, second largest after the state itself.

"We have used games and gambling to redistribute wealth for centuries if not millennia," she wrote in *History News*, the publication of the American Association of State and Local History, in 2001. "Get used to it."

After all, William Clark, approaching the Umatilla area in April 1806 on the way back to St. Louis, wrote: "I observed another game which these people also play; it is played by 2 persons with 4 sticks about the Size of a man's finger and about 7 inches in length. . . . The man who is in possession of the Sticks &c places them in defferent positions, and the opposit party tels the position of the black Sticks by a motion of either or both of his hands."

The Stick Game in its classical version may not be offered at the Wild Horse casino, but the principle is there.

Conner's directness—and a fierce and focused flow of language that leaves the most casually encountered journalist fumbling for his notebook—makes her a formidable figure and organizational infighter. She is relentless in running a meeting.

"She can be incredibly tough," says Sammye Meadows, who has spent years working with Conner on the Circle of Tribal Advisors. "She can bring people to tears. She has such a command of language, that people can't respond."

Conner, a blunt-cut woman with explosively curling black hair, offers an unblinkingly clear-eyed view of any situation.

"We have a lot of experience," she told a workshop on bicentennial tribal involvement in Great Falls, Montana, in the spring of 2003, "with people lying to us."

And while Lewis and Clark event planners might be designing photo opportunities, Conner reminded the group, "We're rebuilding nations. Our definition of success may not be the same as yours."

Local groups trying to work with tribes should know, she warned, that "people are putting out other fires. Your crisis will not go to the top of our list."

And always, "'Don't try to censor tribal speech. That will kill your relationship in a heartbeat."

By then, Conner had already spent five years putting out bicentennial fires, not to mention starting some. She starting going to Lewis and Clark meetings in 1998 and at the outset didn't see what tribes would get out of it. After attending several meetings of the emerging Circle of Tribal Advisors, she was elected to its board in 1999.

"It surprised me," she remembers. "I didn't know I was running for the board."

Over the next few years—in meetings from Louisville, Kentucky, to Lewiston, Idaho—Conner did a stint as chairman of the rapidly growing COTA. She joined the national Bicentennial Council, where her tribal and bureaucratic bilingualism made her council secretary and then vice president.

At every point, she made it clear that the story wasn't just about Lewis and Clark, but about the people who met them.

"We are numerous, we are diverse and we still populate this land," she said, preparing for the opening ceremonies of the National Museum of the American Indian in September 2004. "We are still here. There are small nations and larger nations, but we are still here."

Conner was baffled when media people wanted to talk to her only about tribal anger and bitterness. Expressing rage and resentment was easy, she knew, but how was anything productive supposed to come out of that? To Conner, the bicentennial was an opportunity for a Umatilla agenda— to call attention to the tribes' rights under the 1855 treaty, the fishing rights and land accesses the tribes were promised in exchange for their land, and their calling to protect all the lands in the upper Columbia Basin.

What bothered her about the opening event at Monticello had nothing to do with Indian-white conflict but with dozens of senior tribal members—from all along the trail—deposited into a snowy and freezing Virginia in January.

"We felt really horrible," Conner said months later, still visibly upset, "because we didn't take good care of our elders at Monticello."

Bureaucratic infighting rolled off her back; leaving tribal elders vulnerable left a mark.

Over the first two years of the bicentennial, with every event along the trail a new situation, a new negotiation, Conner saw some progress, some complications. "It's not instinctive. This is a labored effort," she said in mid-2004. "We're learning a lot about cross-cultural cooperation."

Some events went better than others. What especially annoyed Conner were occasions when local politicians would be lengthily introduced and tribal officials ignored.

"We like to do formal introductions," she once noted. "If anybody does pomp and circumstance well, it's Indians."

The last night of the Monticello kickoff, Sammye Meadows remembers, the Indians who came to the event had an impromptu dance explosion back at the University of Virginia. Still in their ceremonial regalia from the formal event that afternoon, the dancers were having such a good time that many of them—including Conner—ended up being late to the closing reception, sponsored by the Lewis and Clark Trail Heritage Foundation and government agencies.

Being late, said Meadows, Conner didn't hear cautionary remarks to the gathering by Secretary of the Interior Gale Norton that the bicentennial should not put too much emphasis on Indians. Of course, it's hard to think Conner would have cared if she had.

When Conner did arrive, recalled Meadows, "Bobbie, as usual, just walked in and took charge without asking anybody. She began doing a mega-Indian giveaway, congratulating and thanking everyone."

Coming right after Norton's remarks, says Meadows, "It was embarrassing.

"But we were also sort of pleased about it."

Three

Returning to the Land

In early June 1805, the way natural historian Daniel Botkin tells the story, Lewis and Clark came to a fork in the Missouri River in south-central Montana. If they started up the wrong waterway, they might run out of summer and never make it across the Rockies that year. The captains spent two days walking up the two rivers, thinking about the advice they had gotten from the tribes and figuring out the most crucial decision on the trip so far.

During those days, long days of hoping for an answer and looking out for grizzlies, days when the entire expedition hung in the balance, Lewis and Clark carefully identified and described three new species of birds.

That episode was part of a stunning, previously unimaginable legacy of the Corps of Discovery—a precise description of 300 species of animals and plants previously unknown to science and to scientific classification. For centuries, explorers typically had sent back samples or promises of wealth—gold or furs or spices. From their first stop, the winter spent in the Mandan villages of North Dakota, Lewis and Clark sent President Thomas Jefferson a live prairie dog.

Jefferson seemed to consider it a very thoughtful gift.

Wherever they went, whatever their circumstances, Lewis and Clark described what they found, drawing on Lewis' compressed naturalist training at Philadelphia and on the volumes they dragged back and forth across a continent. "Lewis," explains Professor Gary Moulton of the University of Nebraska, editor of the new multi-volume journals of the expedition, "was blessed with the qualities most important in a naturalist; an unquenchable curiosity, keen observational powers, and a systematic approach to understanding the natural world."

Nobody ever said that about the conquistadors.

The two captains carefully selected plant specimens—still preserved at the American Philosophical Society at Philadelphia—some of which, 200 years later, became part of the Lewis and Clark bicentennial traveling exhibit. They crafted the accounts of their discoveries in language many might find unusual for wilderness pioneers.

"I also met with great numbers of Grouse or Prarie hens, as

they are called by the English traders of the N.W.," Lewis wrote one day in April 1805, at the far reaches of the unexplored Missouri. "These birds appear to be mating; the note of the male is kuck, kuck, kuck, coo, coo, coo. the first part of the note both male and female use when flying. the male also drums something like the pheasant, but by no means as loud."

In the 19th century, when Americans and foreign tourists would shoot down thousands of buffalo for sport, or for their tongues, or just to starve the Indians who depended on the herds, the captains' naturalist skills didn't exactly resonate. But now, when a number of the creatures on Lewis and Clark's list are on other lists—the threatened and endangered species lists—the captains seem to be explorers as much for our time as theirs.

From salmon runs to grizzly bears, to a prairie that once covered half a continent and now survives in subdivided slices, Lewis and Clark would not recognize their West today—even allowing for the difference in view between a keelboat and a Winnebago. The vast buffalo herds are gone, and the grizzlies are down from an estimated 100,000 to about 1,000. From the huge dams built to drive and domesticate the massive river at the core of Lewis and Clark's mission, giant transmission towers march across the prairie like science-fiction invaders from a Spielbergian mother ship.

And yet, along the thousands of miles of trail stretching west of St. Louis, there is still territory to treasure, territory to evoke the past, territory still worth fighting over. Dr. John Osborn, the Sierra Club activist from Spokane who drove the idea of the club's involvement in the bicentennial, remembers vanished fleets of salmon pounding up the center of the Columbia River in the 1960s. He insists, "You can still see vestiges of it. There are places on the trail where you can look 360 degrees and not see a clear-cut."

That standard may not be lyrical, but in the American West it's notable.

To filmmaker Ken Burns, the test of remaining wilderness is equally modest: "Places without cattle tags or missile silos."

Most importantly to Burns, there are places with opportunity, places that could help reconnect Americans and their history: "The celebration provides some leverage for people to feel a sense of ownership. It might help to foster a greater respect for the land, and the 50 or so other nations [Lewis and Clark] traveled through."

Respect for the land—awe about the land—flows out of the Lewis and Clark journals, bringing a piercing vision of what's lost and what's left. It is what makes two 200-year-old explorers—one of them a slaveholder and Indian remover, the other a manic depressive who disintegrated soon after his return from the wilderness—iconic figures to the delicately developed sensibilities of 21st-century environmentalists.

"Lewis and Clark were better observers of nature and understood it better than most of us today," Botkin explains. "They never would have survived if they hadn't understood nature."

And they could never have described it so vividly if they hadn't delighted in it.

As Clark wrote in his journal in June 1804, just a month into the trip, at a time when he didn't know if he or the journal would survive—"I saw great numbers of deer in the prairies, the evening is cloudy, our party in high spirits."

That kind of spirit about the natural world flows out of the journals and seemed to make the bicentennial an opportunity for a sizable reconsideration of the land the Corps of Discovery covered.

"Somehow," said Bicentennial Council President Robert Archibald, "we'd like the world to be a bit different when we finish this, with more hope for the future. We'd like Americans to feel a little differently about the land and its people than they did 10 years ago."

Or, in the view of Scott Chapman, a Sierra Club volunteer from Portland who traveled to Washington, D.C., to lobby for a Lewis and Clark environmental agenda, "If we miss this opportunity, the tercentennial will be held on a little patch of land."

One of Chapman's allies, Kathryn Hohman of Bozeman, Montana, put it even more bluntly: "We just want to make sure this isn't just about toilet seats and visitors centers."

Before the bicentennial had ever moved into high gear or touched the consciousness of most Americans, the possibilities of the commemoration had reached the classically sensitive political antennae of President Bill Clinton. There is no part of the trail more dramatic, or possibly more untouched—partly because it's not much easier to get there now than it was in 1805—than the Missouri Breaks, a stretch of jagged cliffs enfolding the river, unrolling through the center of Montana.

"As we passed on," Lewis wrote as the Corps moved through the area in May 1805, "it Seemed as if those seens of Visionary enchantment would never have an end. . . . I Should have thought that nature had attempted here to rival the human art of Masonry had I not recollected that She had first begun her work. "

The Missouri Breaks had always resisted development, due to the stretch's inaccessibility and challenging geology. The major way to get there has been, in Corps fashion, by floating the river, and a small but growing tourist business developed around boating and rafting. But environmentalists and local landowners still battled over the formal protection for the area.

Three days before the end of his time in office, on January 17, 2001, Clinton declared the area, stretching 149 miles along the Missouri, a national monument, placing it off off-limits to most development. The departing president did it by catching a ride on the Lewis and Clark Trail, salting his proclamation with long quotations from the journals, and emphasizing the area's significance to the mission:

"The area has remained largely unchanged in the nearly 200 years since Meriwether Lewis and William Clark traveled through it on their epic journey," the proclamation declared. ". . . Lewis and Clark first encountered the Breaks country of the monument on their westward leg. In his journal, Clark described the abundant wildlife of the area, including mule deer, elk, and antelope, and on April 29, 1805, the Lewis and Clark expedition recorded the first bighorn sheep observation by non-Indians in North America."

The designation was hugely controversial, with local cattle ranchers, whose herds grazed on some of the territory, particularly upset, along with Montana Governor Judy Martz, who vowed to remove some of the land from the federal designation. Montana's sole congressman, Denny Rehberg, promised legislation to exclude private property from the monument, and George W. Bush's new secretary of the interior, Gale Norton, pledged to reopen the issue, saying of her predecessors, "They didn't work with local property owners, elected officials and other people whose lives were affected. We're committed to building on the principle of respect for property rights."

And yet, four years later, the designation stood.

"I think it's solid, with nothing much to be worried about," said Joe Gutkoski, president of Montana River Action. "This is probably the part of the Lewis and Clark Trail that looks most like it did when Lewis and Clark came through." Which, environmentalists and an increasing number of Montanans felt, was not only significant in itself, but carried a whole range of possibilities for more and more people coming to see it.

A presidential proclamation, issued exactly two years before the first Signature Event, carved out a goal—a Northwest Passage—that, at least for the bicentennial years, Lewis and Clark and environmental protection might go forward together.

By the time of Clinton's proclamation, environmentalists' planning and efforts to integrate their efforts into the larger bicentennial message were far along. The mission was driven by activists such as John Osborn and Oregon's Paul Shively—who recalls sitting around a mountain campfire with Osborn and a bottle of Yukon Jack honey-flavored whisky and considering strategy.

Years later, Osborn still marveled at the possibilities opened by the bicentennial.

"You pick up a phone, you talk to people," said Osborn. "The Lewis and Clark story captures people. It's not like we go looking for the story; the story comes to us."

The Sierra Club was not about to wait for the story to come to it. The club's effort included lobbying, appearances at bicentennial events, trips along the trail, and a torrent of literature. Its agenda extended to more than 30 preservation objectives throughout the trail states, including some hard-to-connect landmarks such as Oregon's Klamath River—about 300 miles from anyplace where Lewis and Clark had ever set foot.

In January 2003, at the Charlottesville, Virginia, kickoff, the Sierra Club hosted a panel discussion and the first showing of its new Lewis and Clark movie. The mood was so intoxicating that Carl Pope, the Sierra Club's executive director, even sounded almost friendly about the Bush administration. "There is an attitude on the part of the federal government," Pope said, "that this is something special, that this is above politics, that this can bring people together."

Along with the Sierra Club, the national environmental group American Rivers launched its effort to re-create Missouri and Columbia-Snake river systems that "Lewis and Clark would have recognized." That meant challenging the management of the Missouri, which environmentalists charged was run for the benefit of the downriver barge traffic. At the other end of the trail, it meant a drive to breach four Snake River dams that activists blame for crippling the Idaho salmon runs. The proposal, always a long shot, was flatly rejected by the Bush administration at the end of 2004—although a June 2005 court decision seemed to put the idea back on the table.

But American Rivers had political allies in the upper reaches of the Missouri, where elected officials and tourism advocates not only cherished the Lewis and Clark opportunity but also complained that their stretches of the river—and the dam-created lakes—were being drained to raise the river level to support barging in the lower river.

To accompany the Circle of Tribal Advisors (COTA) and the Circle of State Advisors (COSA), the Bicentennial Council created a Circle of Conservation Advisors (COCA).

In 2003, American Rivers' Rebecca Wodder was named to the Bicentennial Council, with a direct mandate: "I was specifically asked to play a leading role in making sure the conservation message came through loud and clear."

And the major national groups picked up local organizational support, from the Ohio River to Northwest salmon advocates. By summer 2005, the Circle of Conservation Advisors claimed 60 organizational members, from the Greater Yellowstone Coalition to the Beargrass Creek Watershed Stakeholders Committee to the Lewis and Clark Trail Heritage Foundation—not by its nature an environmental group.

Its primary drive in Oregon sought federal purchase of some land parcels in one of the most stunning parts of the Lewis and Clark Trail, the Columbia Gorge—a spectacular stretch running east of Portland, where a massive river runs between towering hills and cliffs. It worked closely with a local environmental group, Friends of the Columbia

Gorge, whose founder and matriarch, Nancy Russell, appeared prominently in the Sierra Club Lewis and Clark movie unveiled at Monticello. The goal was to get 4,000 acres purchased, as two timetables ticked together—the bicentennial and a 2004 deadline for the government to purchase some lands or lose its first buyer rights.

The Friends had been working to preserve the Gorge for two decades, but the bicentennial raised the stakes. By 2005, as the commemoration approached the Northwest, the Forest Service had acquired more than 2,000 acres in the Gorge, with a few more parcel possibilities in the pipeline.

"People want to stand where Lewis and Clark stood, and see what they described in their journals," says Tiffany Kenslow, who worked for Friends in The Dalles, about 80 miles upriver from Portland—where she was also a board member of the Columbia Gorge Discovery Center.

"Are they going to see what Lewis and Clark saw, or are they going to see development, logging and maybe some mining?"

Full-time activists setting out to make a bicentennial-based environmental appeal might be predictable. What's striking—and maybe more significant—is how land "stewardship" became a major theme of the mainstream bicentennial effort. What's equally striking is how hard that once was to imagine—especially among historically minded Lewis and Clark fans nervous about anything controversial.

At one early council meeting in North Dakota, recalls David Nicandri, head of the Washington State Historical Society and the state's bicentennial effort, the offer of involvement from American Rivers "survived only because Stephen Ambrose spoke up for it. It took the power of the great Lewis and Clark man himself to pass it."

Since then, marvels Nicandri, "The environmental message has greater and greater acceptance in the Lewis and Clark world. Early on, we heard some tribal resistance; people thought it might pre-empt the Native American story."

But by the time the Signature Events began, it seemed the tribal and environmental messages—both about preservation of endangered heritages—sometimes dovetailed. Oregon's Confederated Tribes of the Umatilla Indian Reservation, with an economic and religious focus on salmon preservation, claimed a mission as land and wildlife advocate throughout their traditional Northwest territory, including lands long gone from tribal control. At Monticello, Darrell Martin of Montana's Gros Ventre tribe appeared on both tribal and environmentalist panels—appropriately for a leader of a tribe cultivating a major buffalo herd.

"I'm very interested in the intersection between the tribal connection and the conservation connection," said American Rivers' Wodder after years of her bicentennial efforts. "I think there's a natural fit, salmon being a great example. We're talking about joint PSAs [public service announcements]." By 2005, the idea seemed to be approaching reality.

Over years of planning and preparation, the environmental message—or, as the Bicentennial Council liked to put it, "stewardship"—gained a prominence hard to envision at the beginning.

"It would have been unimaginable, in 1996, '97, '98," says Nicandri, "for a conservation organization person to be one of the half-dozen people shaping the entire message." But somehow, the small bicentennial message group working with the Ad Council—devising a Lewis and Clark message to appear on television, radio, and print advertising spots over three years—included the Sierra Club's Mary Kiesau and a general conservation consensus.

Which did not make it an easy message to craft.

In a hotel meeting room at the Best Western Convention Center in Great Falls, Montana, a fish that no longer jumps in the rivers came leaping off the screen. At the spring 2003 meeting of the national Lewis and Clark Bicentennial Council, Robert Archibald was showing slides to state tourism officials, covering the early inspiration of the Ad Council.

Archibald began by explaining, as he had to every Lewis and Clark interest group and subcommittee he had spoken to over the previous three days, that the Ad Council spots themselves were not educational. The point was just to grab the viewer's interest and direct him or her to the bicentennial's web site. Listeners nodded, without even much wariness.

As the slides began, the tourism officials liked the campaign's catchphrase: "Walk with them and see what you discover." They loved the TV spot with actor Samuel L. Jackson talking about the entire expedition voting on whether to winter north or south of the Columbia, described by Stephen Ambrose in *Undaunted Courage* as "the first time in American history that a black slave had voted, the first time a woman had voted."

Then the screen filled with Clark's precise drawing of a coho salmon, from a run now ruled extinct, with the caption, "Even today their words and sketches can almost bring it to life. Too bad nothing else can."

For a dead fish, it could bite.

"Some of our most supportive people have been from local forest- and food-product corporations," worried Lorraine Roach, a business consultant from Grangeville, Idaho, and local bicentennial organizer. "If we get too provocative, we might alienate people we need."

Idaho's congressional delegation strongly supported the state's bicentennial program, pointed out Keith Peterson, the state coordinator, and the spot might be a problem for them.

"I don't have a problem with land stewardship," he said later. "I just don't want the council's campaign to get into issues like dams and endangered species." And in Idaho, he noted, an extinct fish was code for Snake River dam removal.

Carl Wilgus, the state's tourism director, said of the advertising professionals who designed the ad, "They are a group of Generation Xers living on Manhattan Island, and they're trying to develop a vision, and there's a lot of conflict on the conference calls." Suddenly, officials started to worry that the whole ad campaign might be anti-tourism.

Having a national message about land stewardship as part of a sophisticated, years-long bicentennial ad campaign could be powerful. But devising it could also be extremely complicated. Creating a powerful but acceptable ad about stewardship would take many more conflicted conference calls.

It turned out that asking the Ad Council to throw the fish ad back wasn't even controversial. It seemed the Sierra Club and other environmentalists didn't like it, either. They thought an ad focused on an extinct species would seem defeatist, as though there were no hope remaining.

In the first year of Ad Council spots, and deep into the second, there would be no environmental-themed entry. Later rounds of the TV and radio public-service spots would get to the stewardship message, although they never got to universal approval.

"As in anything, I would like to see a stronger message," admitted Wodder. "The ads are no longer just, 'Woe is me, all is lost.' They have a more positive tone—and I think they could go further."

But if stewardship became a more prominent bicentennial message than observers might have expected in the 1990s, disagreements and disappointing fund-raising limited what its advocates hoped to achieve. Political and economic changes unforeseen in the 1990s cut away at organizational possibilities, even as efforts by the Sierra Club, American Rivers, and the Circle of Conservation Advisors raised public interest.

As Lewis and Clark could tell them, you never know what's around the bend.

Although the environmentalists became a significant voice in the bicentennial, they and the council had a hard time raising money to fund their programs. Foundation money helped elevate the tribal agenda, and corporate giving bolstered some local events, but nobody seemed eager to pay for the stewardship message—although Archibald tried hard to find a sponsor.

"There was such a risk of this being a corporate sponsorship deal, and I think we've pulled a lot of that away," the Sierra Club's Shively said with satisfaction, but the absence of eager corporate funders actually limited the stewardship message.

For an early Signature Event, at Louisville in October 2003, the Bicentennial Council and environmental groups managed to put together a pilot program, with a local town-hall meeting on environmental issues, a bus-and-boat tour of nearby Ohio River sites, and a cocktail reception to highlight and honor environmental activists. But without sponsorship or other fund-raising surges, the Bicentennial Council couldn't manage to repeat such activities in the 2004 Signature Events.

"We didn't end up with the kind of budget that we'd hoped. COCA has been operating pretty much on a shoestring," concluded Wodder in June 2005. "It's been a great grass-roots effort. I think it could have been more national."

Still, between a national media campaign and the grass-roots effort, "If I had to pick one, I would have picked the one we've got." The effort claimed a success, Wodder said, in "getting the people who live along the trail to understand their connection to it."

By the end of that year, booming sales of bicentennial commemorative coins—the 500,000 sets that were minted moved quickly—produced money not only to pay off the council's debts, but to underwrite more environmental activities at the 2005-2006 events. As the trail moved through Montana to the Pacific and back, programs would extend to more conservation speakers, excursions to neighboring areas of environmental concern, and connections to local conservation groups.

To the explorers who carefully noted the difference between the drumming of the newly encountered prairie hen and the eastern pheasant—and who negotiated their way among newly encountered tribes by handing out large medals with Thomas Jefferson on them—that outcome might have made sense.

But the national economic decline that began in 2000, which gathered force after 9/11, cut away at the federal government's ability to spend money in support of the bicentennial and land purchases, and Republican control over of the White House and then the entire Congress cut back on its willingness to do so.

As Representative Brian Baird (D-Wash.), a leader of Congress' Lewis and Clark Caucus, recalled, early plans called for a $500 million federal bicentennial budget. In August 2001, Senator Joe Lieberman of Connecticut—the 2000 Democratic vice-presidential candidate and 2004 presidential hopeful—called for a strong federal bicentennial effort, declaring, "If they could travel 8,000 miles through unknown territory, the least we can do is go the extra mile to ensure that their monumental journey is properly commemorated." (The Capitol Hill newspaper *Roll Call* immediately envisioned the campaign button: "Lieberman '04, a Voyage of Discovery.")

After the attacks on the World Trade Center and the Pentagon, resources and focus both faded. A tentatively planned meeting between Representative Doug Bereuter (R-Neb.)—a bicentennial advocate for a decade—and Vice President Dick Cheney never made it onto the vice-presidential schedule.

Involvement by federal agencies, notably the National Park Service and the Interior Department in general, helped keep the bicentennial together when it had not much else going for it. But observers noted that some of the agencies were particularly nervous about the prominence of the Sierra Club.

"I think there's a way to express that message," carefully explained Michelle Dawson, a spokesperson for the Bureau of Land Management, at one Lewis and Clark gathering, "without being quite so negative about it."

Some of the figures most powerful in the new Washington, D.C., including people most directly interested in Lewis and Clark, didn't think new federal land acquisition was the right way to go. To some westerners, the Lewis and Clark expedition was one of the last acceptable federal programs in the region.

In his Washington, D.C., office, Senator Larry Craig (R-Idaho) proudly and gently displayed one of the blue beads brought by Lewis and Clark to trade with the tribes. The bead, he said with a tinge of embarrassment, probably came out of a gravesite. He also showed off a model of William Clark's traveling fold-open writing surface, calling it "Clark's laptop."

Craig, also a caucus member, recalled, "I've been a buff of Lewis and Clark most of my life." He started reading the journals in eighth grade and had been out on the trail for a day with Ambrose—the next best thing to traveling with the Corps itself.

But that didn't mean the powerful senior Republican—chairman of the Public Lands and Forests subcommittee and a high-ranking member of the Appropriations Committee—was buying into any bicentennial conservation agenda.

"I'm certainly willing to look at all of that," he says. "It's interesting they want to protect something that's reasonably well protected. Apparently, it's been well taken care of over 200 years."

Still, as the bicentennial moved into its highest-profile times, legitimate Lewis and Clark environmental possibilities emerged. The highest-profile project was the proposed Lewis and Clark Mount Hood Wilderness Act, introduced by Senator Ron Wyden (D-Ore.) to cover another 177,000 acres, including places along the Columbia River that figured in the expedition's story.

"The bicentennial is going to generate more attention and interest," explained Wyden, "and that can only be a plus for those of us trying to build a bipartisan consensus."

The immediate response to Wyden's bill was tepid, but he declared his willingness to keep it alive and adapt it to objections. "We're really pleased to see it," said the Sierra Club's Mary Kiesau. "The bill needs some work, but it's a really strong and workable conservation bill."

In North Dakota, the Sierra Club worked with the Mandan-Hidatsa-Arikara Nation to increase the level of protection of several trail sites along the Missouri. The state's U.S. senators expressed interest in the idea. From Missouri to Washington state, locals and lobbyists have lists of Lewis and Clark locations and legislative agendas.

"A lot of interesting things are happening," declared Kiesau. "In states like Montana, North Dakota, South Dakota, that usually don't see environmental things at the state level, we're seeing some things happen.

"Tying in Lewis and Clark to conservation does make sense to people. It's not just about a lot of issues, it's about finding a new way to talk to people."

I have been as wet and as cold in every part," William Clark wrote in his journal on September 16, 1805, "as I have ever been in my life."

In just about the same place where he wrote that, you can still have that feeling.

It's a short stretch, where Montana crosses into Idaho, up around the Gem State's northern neck. Among Lewis and Clark buffs, the Lolo Pass may be the most sacred stretch of the trail, and it makes a powerful argument about protecting the lands of Lewis and Clark—not because it's a place that's endangered, but because it's a place where 1805 speaks directly to us.

A little farther down Highway 12—the Lewis and Clark Highway—there's a hillock called Heart of the Monster, where a Nez Perce creation story described a huge creature coming out of the Earth. The Lolo Pass is almost as central to the Lewis and Clark creation story.

Most obviously, Highway 12 itself is a display of the stunning—if rarely easily accessible—natural glory the Lewis and Clark expedition experienced. It runs across the neck of Idaho from Missoula, Montana, to Clarkston, Washington, through the Bitterroot Mountain range, alongside the Lochsa River, and then beside the Clearwater River, a stream that has never made anybody wonder how it got its name.

It is a narrow pass through towering heights, with the road aiming directly toward thousand-foot walls of trees, until seemingly at the last moment the road shifts left or right. The winding, sinuous stretch extends for about 200 miles, but it runs longer because you keep stopping to gape.

It also has large numbers of the brown-and-white Lewis and Clark road signs indicating that the explorers trudged here, although in fact they did not. They took a much tougher road, up on the ridge overlooking the highway, the place where Clark was freezing and where people traveling in his steps are reverent.

"The road through this hilley Countrey is very bad passing over hills & thro' Steep hollows, over falling timber, &c. &c.," wrote Clark in September 1805, sounding like he was trying to keep from falling over himself. "Continued on & passed Some most intolerable road on the Sides of the Steep Stony mountains, which might be avoided by keeping up the Creek, which is thickly covered with under growth & falling timber."

Their path is now called the Lolo Motorway, and it is a combination of historical monument, wilderness trail, and practical joke. According to the federal government—which graded the trail a long time ago and then decided that a leveled-out trail was no fun—the motorway is best traversed by horse or mountain bike and by no mechanized vehicle less rugged than a Hummer, assuming you can't get hold of a tank. Should you try it in, say, a Buick, warns the U.S. Forest Service, "tow truck service can take days to arrange and cost $250-$500."

As Dayton Duncan points out, the stretches that were tough for Lewis and Clark are still tough for us.

It's all described in the Forest Service's chilling but deadpan handout, "Driving the Lolo Motorway," which reads like a Stephen King effort at nonfiction. However you travel the motorway, it's a rugged trip—although in 2002, the Forest Service did request bids for installing log toilets.

"Despite what we tell them, most people don't believe how rough the road is until they get on it and realize they can't go much faster than 10 mph," Kris Perry, Clearwater National Forest Lewis and Clark Bicentennial programs coordinator, told the Spokane *Spokesman-Review*. "It takes a good nine hours to drive the route."

Or several days to be towed out.

Still, approaching the bicentennial, the Forest Service set up a lottery for permits, because it expected more people would want to travel—or try to travel—the Lolo Motorway than the agency thought plausible. The demand was lower than expected, or feared, although some tourists still wanted to try out the all-terrain vehicle they got for Christmas. But a number of them—including some who have tried it in the past—see the Lolo Pass as the place to come closest to the Lewis and Clark experience.

"You can't do what Christopher Columbus did. You can't do what Neil Armstrong did," David Borlaug, head of the North Dakota bicentennial effort and an early president of the national Bicentennial Council, once explained. "You can do pretty close to what Lewis and Clark did. It's people's own sense of adventure."

Lately, there hasn't been much logging in the Lolo area, but protecting it is one of the Sierra Club goals—although, given the local political atmosphere, perhaps one of its less likely goals. "In this great national museum, the last wilderness section of the entire trail is the Lochsa River country," said John Osborn. "It's remote, it's wild, it's incredible and it's a real national treasure."

The Northern Rockies chapter of the Sierra Club calls for the federal government to include all of the Lolo Trail in the Nez Perce Historic Trail Park. The Nez Perce and Lewis and Clark Trails would run across each other in yet another way.

In May 2005, a coalition of environmental groups, including the Lands Council of Spokane, founded in 1983 by Osborn, sued the Forest Service to prevent logging on 117 acres visible from the Lolo Trail. They argued that the time of the bicentennial was a particularly inappropriate time to log near the trail. "We felt the historic nature and the values were sort of given short shrift," Gary Macfarlane of Friends of the Clearwater told the Associated Press. "One would hope the agency would have given a little more credence and concern to part of our cultural heritage."

But even if it never surges up onto any legislative calendar, the Lolo territory is at the core of the Lewis and Clark conservation theme. It's a place, 200 years of history and development later, that still captures the sense of wildness, the feel of an open land with grizzlies, old growth, and possibility.

Just a bit east, still in the Rockies in August 1805, Meriwether Lewis sealed a new friendship with a Montana tribal chief by an exchange of clothing and wrote in his journal that wearing the chief's buckskin shirt left him "metamorphosed," a Virginia gentleman suddenly turned into a mountain man.

"Just for a moment, Meriwether Lewis saw himself as a part of the natural world," Archibald says of the clothing swap. "This is a moment when we could join Meriwether Lewis and imagine how the world, and us, could be different if we became wild for just a moment."

And Lolo could be both the place for it and an argument for it.

Sitting in a Portland restaurant, on a flying visit to Oregon to pump up turnout before the 2004 election, Sierra Club Executive Director Carl Pope looked up from his salmon hash and considered his organization's investment in Lewis and Clark.

"I don't think the numbers the Commerce Department projected are actually panning out," he concluded about projections of vast numbers of tourists journeying along the trail, already fading among bicentennial planners.

"As a long-term effort to get Americans connected to the landscape, it's not doing as well as we expected. It's a single, not a home run. But the delegations, including people we don't work with that often, are excited. It's done better as a policy vehicle than I thought. We've actually got viable legislative vehicles that are actually moving."

As commemorations go, that outcome isn't a bad evocation of Lewis and Clark at all. After all, hardly any settler or trader ever followed a literal route; even on the way back, Lewis admitted to himself that few goods could profitably follow the trail they were blazing.

The triumph of the expedition wasn't creating a new trail, but creating a new West. If Lewis and Clark didn't discover a lucrative short cut to the Pacific, they did discover an ecosystem—a word they never knew and certainly couldn't have spelled—of creatures, plants, and geology unknown anywhere else in the world.

The captains themselves might have appreciated a bicentennial legacy focused not so much on the trail that they never discovered as on the amazing world that they actually found.

Profile

Mary Kiesau

The goal of the Corps of Exploration was to find a water route to the Pacific, and the boats passing down Seattle's Ballard Canal were just a few miles from the ocean. But the polished, high-tech-financed yachts gliding down to the canal to the sea—or at least to Puget Sound—were more about cocktails than commerce. Far from bringing the harvest of yeoman farmers to market, they were carrying periodontists who live closer to a Porsche than a plow.

Even Thomas Jefferson's forecasts could be off a bit.

Mary Kiesau, sitting on a bench on the bank, knew about the West turning out differently than expected. She was the project manager of the Sierra Club's largest initiative ever, "Wild America: Protecting the Lands of Lewis and Clark," an eight-year effort to seize the bicentennial's momentum for environmental projects. The program included congressional lobbying, a Missouri River of publications and priorities, a Sierra Club presence at all bicentennial events, and a promotion of a sense of the Lewis and Clark journals that looks between the lines to a western landscape now virtually vanished.

"We go to Lewis and Clark events, and people constantly tell us how grateful they are that it gives the bicentennial more value," Kiesau said as the yachts slipped by. "We have our sense of the love of the land, and Lewis and Clark had that same attachment. Their sense of awe at the natural world brings that back out in us. People want that back."

If preservation and restoration seem to crash against the major economic development strategies pushed by chambers of commerce and local boosters all along the trail, Kiesau didn't see it that way.

"It's a big economic opportunity, and there's nothing wrong with that," says Kiesau, watching the yachts, poster products of economic opportunity, cruise along the canal. "No one's going to want to travel anywhere the land's been trashed, if you're driving the SUV and there's nothing pretty to look at."

For years, at gatherings of Lewis and Clark planners, Kiesau was often the youngest person in the room. She sat in blue jeans with quadruply pierced ears and a mammoth backpack at her feet, idly twisting up her long blond hair as commission members discussed office budgets and corporate sponsorships. But she spoke to her fellow planners, in tones of vague nervousness and clear determination, as the voice of the only national political force in the room.

She knows, at this Montana meeting in 2003, that some of the people at the table, especially the Lewis and Clark traditionalists, are nervous about a prominent role in the bicentennial for an activist group.

"We will do it on our own if we have to," she tells them. "We'd prefer to do it with you." When the leader of the oldest Lewis and Clark group declares that he's not going to be part of anything political, she answers evenly, "We don't expect you to. But there's a hell of a lot you can do. There's a lot of space between pushing up against your comfort level and doing nothing."

Kiesau didn't ever plan to do nothing. "It's always been very important to me," she said, "that I don't exist in this world like a robot."

She grew up in North Carolina, where she was "always outside playing with bugs and rodents." She graduated from the University of North Carolina at Chapel Hill with a degree in exercise physiology, which kept broadening out as she pursued it: "Not just eating right and staying fit, but everything combined, such as, what watershed do you drink from?"

After graduating, Kiesau worked as a personal trainer, an emergency medical technician, and a park ranger in Scotland before going from Sierra Club volunteer to employee. For years, she worked on North Carolina issues of urban sprawl and burgeoning pig farms: "There are more pigs in North Carolina than people, and they poop a lot more than people do."

With that situation possibly contributing to her interest in a change of atmosphere, Kiesau was handpicked to direct the Sierra Club's Lewis and Clark effort.

"She knew the structure of the Club, and had a pretty substantial amount of organizing experience in North Carolina," said Bill Arthur, now the Sierra Club's deputy national field director. "She knew how to run a statewide organizing project."

To Arthur, Kiesau offered the skills for the very different demands of directing the club's Lewis and Clark effort.

"One of the things we saw as an opportunity and a challenge was working within the larger situation of the bicentennial commission," he says. "At the same time, we are an advocacy group, trying to leverage a specific discussion. There's some potential tension there. Your agenda may not be what they want to do. I think she did a good job of dancing that line."

In the Lewis and Clark world, dancing is a fairly freighted metaphor, carrying images of the expedition members dancing at campfire to Pierre Cruzette's fiddle, often using the occasion to break down barriers with local tribes. From Virginia across the continent, Kiesau has done a considerable amount of that kind of dancing.

She was part of planning at the Bicentennial Council meetings and personally staffed the Sierra Club booth at the Monticello opening event in January 2003. Kiesau worked on a bus-and-riverboat environmental overview at the bicentennial event in Louisville that October—marking the 200th anniversary of Lewis joining up with Clark—and helped coordinate Sierra Club organizational efforts on all the trail states, including backpack and hiking expeditions. The expeditions were pitched to combine nature appreciation, evoking the spirit of Lewis and Clark, and serious lobbying for Sierra Club legislative goals in each area.

The treks were a kind of re-creation of Kiesau's own college emphasis: exercise, eating, and environmentalism.

To meetings of the Bicentennial Council, Kiesau brought the resources of a national group of hundreds of thousands, a clear agenda, and an organizational and media savvy beyond most in the room. At the meeting where representatives of state organizations talked about their plans for a press conference on the final day of the Monticello kickoff, she murmured that the Sierra Club would never hold its press conference on a day when other news would overshadow its message.

By that meeting in 2002, Kiesau and the Sierra Club were deep into their national campaign, with some disappointments and some surprising successes. Hit with a national economic downturn, the group had had to cut its budget by three-quarters and hadn't found a financial partner to underwrite its message; one never did appear. But the club had produced a massive wave of publications and priorities, connected with politicians not always eager to be seen with environmentalists, and acquired a considerable crowd of volunteers and activists in the states along the trail.

Still, Kiesau conceded, it was always easier to create activists than to create the right message for them to carry.

The traditional Lewis and Clark enthusiasts seemed to grow a bit less suspicious of the environmentalists' role—although some government agencies never did. But her role in the debate—and on the group advising on the Ad Council message—remained a landmark by itself.

And Kiesau's prominence has also worked for her own group.

"Mary gets the big picture, branding the message," said Paul Shively, of the Sierra Club in Oregon. "You do a Lexis/Nexis search of Lewis and Clark and you'll see a hell of a lot of hits on the Sierra Club. We've done a lot of things to put this on the map as an environmental message."

Oddly, in the course of that happening, something else strange occurred.

"She's really embraced and become an aficionado of the whole Lewis and Clark thing," said Shively. "I've seen her go from going through the motions to someone who really believes the whole thing."

Now, Kiesau's longtime involvement with the outside had another theme to it. "It's great to see the wilderness with Lewis and Clark," she said.

Still, by spring 2005, just as the bicentennial was approaching Kiesau's planning base in the Northwest, it was enough. She quit, leaving the airplane schedules and the Seattle office for a remote valley in central Washington, where she planned to work part-time on an organic farm and do some local organizing.

"This wasn't me any more," Kiesau explained. "I really wanted to live my life out of the office. I am not a city person; it's time to do something else. I want to be better connected to the land."

She would carry out to her own piece of country the parts of the Sierra Club job that weren't in the office, the days canoeing the Missouri and seeing grizzlies in the wild.

"There's a lot of wonder and greatness and amazing beauty in the West, and not a lot of people get to see them," Kiesau said the day before leaving the job. "It feels like it's getting rarer and rarer."

Maybe that's another risk of spending six years reading the Lewis and Clark journals and explaining to half a country that the captains' rapt accounts of a world they'd never imagined carry a message about how 21st-century Americans should lead their lives.

You come to believe it.

Four

The River Runs Through It

From a small boat rolling up America's biggest river, you can see a flock of Canada geese strutting on a pile of rocks. If the boat's motor churns up the water too much, a 12-pound carp might come flying out, with enough force (carp × acceleration) to break a boater's rib.

Everywhere, jutting out from either bank, are rock-lined wing dikes, sticking out into the river to direct water into the navigation channel. And suddenly, just around a bend, is the Kansas City skyline.

"Millions of people every day cross over this river," says Brian Canaday, a policy coordinator for the Missouri Department of Conservation, steering his boat up the river and watching out for jumping carp, "and they hardly ever look at it."

Lewis and Clark, of course, spent more time than they ever wanted looking at the Missouri, fighting it for months from St. Louis to the Montana Rockies, and then cruising back down it in a matter of weeks. It was faster going with the current—although not as fast as it would be now.

Whether, after watching the river all that time, they would recognize it now is another question. With gigantic dams creating massive lakes upriver and wing dikes and the Corps of Engineers channeling it downriver, the Missouri is now a faster, deeper, and in many places straighter river than the one the Corps navigated. The Corps of Discovery's trip up the river would now be impossible, and not just because of locks or the chance of getting run over by a barge. These days, the Missouri runs so fast that rowing, poling, and pulling your way up it is now inconceivable, and even the most scrupulously authentic re-enactors have an engine somewhere inside their carefully handworked hull.

The Lewis and Clark story has always been about rivers, starting at the very beginning with the letter of instruction Thomas Jefferson wrote Meriwether Lewis in June 1803.

"The object of your mission is to explore the Missouri river, & such principal stream of it, as, by it's course & communication with the water of the Pacific Ocean, may offer the most direct & practicable water communication across this continent, for the purposes of commerce . . . ," directed the president. "The interesting points of the portage between the heads of the Missouri & the water offering the best communication with the Pacific Ocean should be fixed by observation, & the course of that water to the ocean, in the same manner as that of the Missouri."

"The water offering the best communication with the Pacific ocean" was, of course, the Columbia. Besides the Missouri, the expedition was about rivers that Jefferson could not name yet, but knew were vital.

The Lewis and Clark river connection runs from that letter to the thousands of Lewis and Clark Trail signs that today trace the course of the Missouri and the Columbia—and the Yellowstone and the Snake.

But for the bicentennial, the rivers are not only in history; they are also in court.

For the past decades, federal courts have been a virtual tributary of the Columbia. Fielding lawsuits from tribes on fishing rights, from environmentalists on species protection, from energy users on the Bonneville Power Administration, and from states alarmed about the federal government and each other, men in black have been largely running the river.

Each new national administration and each new federal policy routes the river back into court. As the bicentennial approached, as the re-enactors came up the Missouri, environmental activists declared that the greatest tribute to Lewis and Clark would be a Columbia with a healthy salmon run and argued for the removal of four eastern Washington dams on the Snake River to re-create the Idaho runs. At the end of 2004, the Bush administration sharply reduced the miles of regional rivers and streams under federal control for salmon protection and declared that the Snake River dams would not be removed. The administration did promise that actions would be taken to make the dams more salmon-friendly—following, of course, the previous instructions of a federal judge.

Salmon supporters declared that they would see the government in court, where the feds already had an appointment with another group of activists—supporters of bull trout, including the Alliance for the Wild Rockies and the Friends of the Wild Swan. In June 2005, federal Judge James Redden rejected the administration's proposal to relax salmon-habitat protection in the basin—saying the proposal was intended not to restore the runs but only to keep the species from extinction—and ordered the government to try again. The administration declared it would appeal the decision.

It's hard to know just how the Corps of Discovery would have felt about their rivers running into court. Jefferson had a notoriously bleak view of federal courts, largely because they had been stacked by his predecessor, John Adams, just before the third president took office. On the other hand, the only building still remaining on the trail that Lewis and Clark actually entered is a courthouse, in Cahokia, Illinois—a courtroom that at least in principle connects to the U.S. Eighth Circuit Court of Appeals, with the power to decide the current identity of the Missouri River.

Beginning in 2002, upriver and downstream states, environmentalists, and the U.S. Army Corps of Engineers battled in three federal courts about the level of the Missouri—whether it flows for the piping plovers, the pallid sturgeon, and upriver recreation or the downriver traffic of grain barges.

The Missouri, draining a huge hunk of continent, is a different river to different people in different places. From Sioux City, Iowa, to St. Louis, it is a working river with a barge traffic—although a diminishing one—and its downriver leaders want a high summer water level to keep the traffic going. Upriver, in the Dakotas and Montana, it is a massive power generator, and water power's side-effect of huge lakes and reservoirs drives a major recreation industry that needs a water level that reaches the sailboat and Ski-Doo docks.

To environmentalists, it is a resource that needs to be managed for the benefit of the river's own population, the fish and water birds that consider the Missouri their permanent home—and for whom home improvement might mean, say, fewer wing dikes and more sandbars.

For all of them, years of drought have raised the stakes and maybe permanently changed the game.

Over all of them is the Army Corps of Engineers, which manages the river like a homeowner with a backyard hose; and over the Corps is Congress—notably powerful Senator Christopher Bond of Missouri, bulwark of the barge industry.

Most powerful of all, sometimes almost inaudibly but always inescapably, is the historic Missouri, running back to Lewis and Clark, a wild river that makes its own course—and changes it when it feels like it.

At one level, it's a water-wonkish argument about river flow. At another level, it's about the role and the future of the Missouri and the seven states it touches.

"There's not enough water for all the uses," says Canaday, Missouri's representative to the Missouri River Natural Resource Conference and the state Conservation Department's liaison to the governor and the legislature. "If we were a Third World country, we'd be (literally) fighting over it. Every person is so passionate about whatever part of the river they work on. They take it very personally."

Canaday often speaks to groups about Lewis and Clark and the river, and he uses the chance to talk about the Missouri's issues and its future. Right now, he says, it's a polarized situation, and he hopes the bicentennial can help open up the discussion and bring together the people who are talking.

It has been a nasty argument, but maybe it's a good time to have it.

"I'm really hopeful, anxious, excited," he says, slowly working his motorboat back from Kansas City to his boat ramp in suburban Sugar Creek. "We want to get the public's attention on this resource. Let them get excited about it."

A lot of people already are.

Even to people who know the river only from the refrain to "Shenandoah"—the part that goes "Across the wiiiiiide Missouri"—the Big Muddy occupies a big space. The Mississippi has magnolias and Mark Twain, but the Missouri, at 2,400 miles from Montana to St. Louis, is the nation's longest and strongest river. The Missouri doesn't run into the Mississippi, declaimed Daniel Webster: "The Missouri seizes the Mississippi and carries it by force to New Orleans." If the United States had been settled eastward from the Pacific, we might think a massive Missouri flowed from the Rockies to the Gulf of Mexico, with a pleasant tributary called the Mississippi joining it from the north.

Going up the Lewis and Clark Trail now, car travelers find themselves repeatedly going back and forth over the river, a crossing always marked by a small green sign with the deadpan announcement, "Missouri River." For a river of its size and meaning, it seems somehow understated. The Missouri merits a marking more dramatic, something like "The Rubicon: Careful When Crossing" or "The Styx: One-Way Traffic Only."

Lewis and Clark had never seen anything like it. Pole or row yourself upriver, and there might suddenly be a sandbar right in your path. Camp on an island, and the river might suddenly decide it wanted it back. The Missouri might have been at the core of their expedition and their hopes for a Northwest Passage, but it was also a huge brown-green beast—later described in western legend as "too thick to drink, too thin to plow"—not open to negotiations.

It was, as Bernard De Voto wrote in *The Course of Empire* in 1952, "swift, hurling its matted debris at any craft that entered it, perilous with snags and boils and sandbags and crumbling banks, the channels to be found only as they were come upon and always changing."

And that was the river running through the plains. When it got to eastern Montana and into the badlands, it stopped being so accommodating.

"The obstructions of rocky points and riffles still continue as yesterday," wrote Meriwether Lewis at the end of May 1805, as the Corps fought its way up the Missouri Breaks. "At those places the men are compelled to be in the water even to the armpits, and the water is yet very could, and so frequent are those point that they are one fourth of their time in the water, added to this the banks and bluffs along which they are obliged to pass are so slippery and the mud so tenacious that they are unable to wear their mockersons, and in that situation draging the heavy burthen of the canoe and walking ocasionally for several hundred yards over the sharp fragments of rocks which tumble from the clifts and garnish the borders of the river."

No wonder that on the way back, William Clark decided to skip that section and catch the Yellowstone east.

To anyone following the Lewis and Clark route today, the change in the Missouri River becomes clear almost immediately, just up from its mouth at Camp Wood. As a traveler moves up the river from St. Louis, the first sign of St. Charles, the town where the expedition departed—then French, now suburban—is a giant floating Ameri-star casino, a strong indication that people still put money into the river.

But the change in the river itself is explained by volunteers just around the bend at the Lewis and Clark Boat House and Nature Center, maintained by an active group of local activists and Corps of Discovery re-enactors. Inside a brick-and-iron-bar structure sit precise replicas of the expedition's keelboat and two canoes.

They sit there, unless they're out on the river. For three years, the boats are at the core of an elaborate two-and-a-half-year expedition re-enactment, which will discover yet again that the Missouri may feel like it goes on forever, but it never reaches the Pacific.

But if the boats are the same—except, of course, for those useful motors—it's a different Missouri.

One day in 2003, Peter Geery—a small, leathery retiree who had wandered down to the river several years before and had suddenly found himself enlisted to sand 40 feet of a re-created keelboat—sat on a bench well up from the bank, thinking about Lewis and Clark and the Missouri.

"When they went through," Gerry said casually, looking at the ground at his feet as though preparing to start treading water, "this was river."

At St. Charles, the Missouri is now 200 yards wide; at Lewis and Clark's departure in 1804, it stretched 780 yards. The river, at least, remembers its former boundaries and every so often sweeps over its new banks with irredentist fury. The boathouse, Geery explained, is built with walls two feet thick, and pillars going down six feet into bedrock—"designed to withstand a runaway barge."

During its many months on the river, the Corps of Discovery had to worry about Sioux and sandbars, but not that.

From the place where Lewis and Clark set out, Geery looked out at a modern river, engineered to congressional and commercial specifications. But he could also look around at the 19th-century village of St. Charles—sometimes called the Williamsburg of the West—and see a huge tourism resource, drawing 1.5 million people a year and attracting tens of thousands of visitors for its spring 2004 Signature Event.

Geery didn't see that weekend. After retiring to St. Charles, near his wife's family, and becoming an avid re-enactor—he gave out business cards for both his family's bed-and-breakfast and for himself in his Corps uniform as Sergeant John Ordway—Geery died a few months before the bicentennial reached his town.

The Signature Event featured re-enactor Corps members from all around the Midwest. Many of them, along with period craftsmen in leather and pottery and iron, settled and camped on the grassy acres along the riverbanks.

Inescapably, the event was all about the Missouri—the river that was and the river that still flows through thousands of miles and the national imagination.

"I like to come down here in the evening," Peter Geery said, "and just watch the river."

The first sign that Lewis and Clark had made it over the Continental Divide, that they were on what could be called (extremely loosely) the downhill run, was a piece of salmon served them by the Lemhi Shoshone in Idaho. "This was the first salmon I had seen," wrote Lewis, "and perfectly convinced me that we were on the waters of the Pacific Ocean."

He was, of course, wrong. The ocean was farther away, and the salmon more adventurous and determined, than Lewis imagined. Moreover, Lewis and Clark never particularly enjoyed salmon—they thought it could never compare with a nice, fresh dog—although they carefully noted salmon's importance to the tribes and, tracing its course up the river, the ways of preserving it and its importance in the local trade. "There was great joy with the nativs last night in consequence of the arrival of the Salmon," wrote Lewis in April 1806; "one of those fish was cought; this was the harbenger of good news to them."

The direct identification of the Columbia with salmon, central to tribes for thousands of years, has run from Lewis' lunch across the 200 years since and has marked the Columbia's course both as a river and as a public policy issue. "Columbia River salmon" has been a culinary cliché, as vast numbers of the rich-fleshed fish have been taken out of the river. Clark found the number of salmon in the Columbia "almost inconceivable," and decades later fisherman would toss nets into the river and then use horses to drag out the huge, flopping catch. In the early 20th century, millions of salmon a year were caught in the Columbia, feeding dozens of canneries on the piers at Astoria.

By the end of the century, the effects of heavy fishing, and of the massive dams on the Columbia and the Snake, had driven the catch down sharply, and several salmon species had virtually disappeared from numerous stretches and streams—including the area around Salmon, Idaho. The catches and seasons were largely set by federal judges, both to help the fish's survival and to take into account tribal treaty fishing rights.

The argument about restoring salmon, about how it can be done and how much is possible, is an endless debate in the Pacific Northwest, with battles among industries relying on the river for power, farmers drawing water from the Columbia for irrigation, and different fishermen battling among themselves. All sides demand that decisions be made based on the best science available, but not many agree on what that would mean. The issues include water level, stream and river habitat protection, and the role of the Snake River dams. Salmon advocates are pushing for the dams' breaching or removal—although political observers think that's about as likely as a Missouri River Lewis and Clark would recognize.

Part of the argument is about the Columbia River that Lewis and Clark visited.

"These are the most pivotal years since the late '60s," says Charles Hudson of the Columbia River Intertribal Fisheries Commission in Portland, a frequent courtroom presence in battles over the river. "The whole idea of a dammed river being an environmental baseline, while tribal fishermen are a threat to the Endangered Species Act, is not going over well with the tribes. It really is a question of who was here first."

In their view of Northwest history, notes Hudson, people start counting at carefully selected times: the arrival of the dams beginning in the 1930s, the Northwest Power agreement of 1960, the rise of Boeing throughout the 20th century. The bicentennial—and the 150th anniversary of the Northwest tribal treaties in 2005—gives the tribes a chance to start counting at a different time.

"We think it will give us a chance to revisit the treaty numbers, of the 11 million to 16 million salmon that once went up the Columbia. We're in the process of excerpting passages from the [expedition] journals to show that. Lewis and Clark chronicled harvests of lampreys, harvests of salmon, in places where they are not any more."

During the Lewis and Clark bicentennial and the years to follow, federal judges are likely to join the many people poring over the Lewis and Clark journals. It beats reading the U.S. Tax Code.

As natural historian Daniel Botkin points out, at the start of the 21st century 36 different governmental bodies had some authority over the salmon of the Pacific Northwest. And just as there was no single authority, there was no single solution. Saving the buffalo, Botkin says, is relatively easy. Saving the salmon is hard.

Still, for the tribes and the many environmental groups in the Northwest, it's the major goal—especially now.

"As America prepares to celebrate the Lewis and Clark bicentennial," declared the Lands Council of Spokane in 1999, "the decisions about the salmon will also be the decisions about the bicentennial— celebration of efforts to restore the river of life, or eulogy for what has been lost in the past 200 years after Lewis and Clark."

John Osborn, founder of the council, still believed in the power of the moment, in the power of moments to change decades.

"When I started this work back in '93 or '94, I had a sense of issues coalescing at the time of the bicentennial," said the Spokane doctor and activist. "I don't think any of that has changed. The Columbia River and its tributary, the Snake, are on a collision course with extinction, occurring at a time when the nation is celebrating the bicentennial. This was an incredible river of life into which those explorers walked. In the blink of an eye—200 years—what has happened?"

At the start of 2005, at a discouraging time for his policy objectives, he still believed that his time was coming—and in the power of the bicentennial.

"We're still focused on the Missouri River side," he said calmly. "All of that changes as of August 12."

On that day in 1805, Lewis wrote: "[The trail] took us to the most distant fountain of the waters of the Mighty Missouri in surch of which we have spent so many toilsome days and wristless nights. thus far I had accomplished one of those great objects on which my mind has been unalterably fixed for many years, judge then of the pleasure I felt in all[a]ying my thirst with this pure and ice-cold water. . . .

"We proceeded on to the top of the dividing ridge from which I discovered immence ranges of high mountains still to the West with their tops partially covered with snow. I now decended the mountain . . . to a handsome bold runing Creek of cold Clear water. here I first tasted the water of the great Columbia river."

At the bicentennial of that moment, said Osborn, the conversation would change.

"I remain confident that stepping across the divide, that event, will rekindle our interest in the Columbia River. It is such a watershed event that I think it will in the end capture the imagination of the people who live in the Northwest."

Maybe it's not visible from space, but it backs up the Missouri River for 134 miles, and you could see that from a long way away.

Lewis and Clark, of course, never saw it at all.

The Fort Peck Dam, over 1,300 miles upriver from St. Charles, is the biggest earth-filled structure in the world, more than 4 miles long and as much as 250 feet high. You can drive along the top of it, but it may not be a great idea if you're susceptible to dizziness or have seen certain disaster movies. The mile-long ride along the top of the dam has a tightrope feel to it, with the deep drop-off of the dam wall on one side and a cliff dive into a 100-mile lake on the other.

You find yourself driving slower and slower.

Fort Peck Dam stretches across and redefines the Missouri. It was the first of the dams that turned the Missouri into a managed river, swelling into huge lakes and then narrowing into swift channels. It is a massive testimony to a nation's frustration with a river that wouldn't behave, the culmination of efforts that began long before anybody imagined such a thing as a hydroelectric dam or home entertainment centers powered by one.

This is not, Daniel Botkin reminds us, a case of a river untouched and eternal until federal bureaucrats got their hands on it. "The Missouri had changed before Lewis and Clark passed its way," says Botkin. "It kept changing under their feet, and it changed after they left."

And then it really started changing.

In 1879, Congress set up the Missouri River Commission to build levees. In 1927, after a huge flood, the Army Corps of Engineers was directed to build dams, locks, and dikes. In 1944, when you would think the federal government might have had other things on its mind, Congress ordered the massive federal project that uprooted tribes, set the upper Missouri states against the lower Missouri states, and left generations of drivers looking nervously from the high-wire heights atop dams into the blue eternity of semi-great lakes.

To the east of Fort Peck Dam, the Missouri rolls out as a streamlined workhorse, more Corps of Engineers than Corps of Discovery. To the west of the lake, through Montana, it often still resembles the cliff-edged, rock-riding river that Lewis and Clark fought their way up with growing astonishment.

From Fort Peck Dam—and from Garrison Dam in North Dakota and Oahe Dam in South Dakota—the power of the Missouri turns on lights for hundreds of miles. The dams also send water down the river, and the bicentennial—along with a lawsuit—again raises the question of how much water.

In Montana and the Dakotas, Republican governors and Democratic senators agree that the Missouri River needs to be run differently.

To people who count on the tourist potential of the lakes, the issue becomes very pointed.

"The commodity economy of the northern Plains, which the river is engineered to serve, is collapsing, and the recreational economy is booming," says Carl Pope of the Sierra Club. Recreation on the upper Missouri is a massively bigger economy than the barge traffic at the other end, which is steadily dropping and carries less than one percent of the region's agricultural output.

But it still has a congressionally mandated claim on the water.

"People in this area worry about conditions in Fort Peck Lake," says Betty Stone, a longtime member of the Montana Lewis and Clark bicentennial commission, at the Cottonwood Inn in Glasgow, a half hour from the dam. "They're getting to be where we're left with boat decks not getting into the water, or marinas that won't work because the water's only four feet deep."

Stone, like most residents of northeast Montana, is not exactly what you'd call an environmentalist. "This area of Montana is very rural," she explains carefully and politely. "We have good stewardship of the land anyway. We probably have less environmental problems than many other areas."

But in her concerns about the Missouri and the way it's operated, she is part of what you might call an unusual alliance.

Charles Kuralt spent years wandering the country for CBS News, becoming one of the best-known and most admired TV newsmen of his time, but what he really wanted to do was write an epic poem about Lewis and Clark. What he actually did, as a board member of American Rivers, was to tell the organization's 1997 national meeting that it should seize the approaching bicentennial to do something about the rivers the explorers traveled.

Two months later, Charles Kuralt was dead. But the organization continued on into what it calls "by far the most ambitious campaign American Rivers has launched in its 25-year history," a voyage of recovery "to restore the rivers of Lewis and Clark." The program involves local organizing, congressional lobbying, and a massive, basketball-court-sized exhibit on the river systems, now in the midst of four years of traveling the country like a multi-media Corps of Explanation.

And, this being 21st-century America, it has also involved litigation. And, this being 21st-century America, the litigation hasn't always turned out predictably.

In 1970, Rebecca Wodder was a high-school civil-rights activist in Omaha when the first Earth Day convinced her there were other issues that needed her. She ended up working for Senator Gaylord Nelson of Wisconsin, the founder of Earth Day, and then—after Nelson lost his Senate seat in the Reagan sweep of 1980—followed him to the Wilderness Society. In 1994, she became president of American Rivers, where she has more than doubled the membership—to 40,000—and opened eight field offices.

"America was settled by rivers," pointed out Wodder. "All of our cities are where they are because of rivers. Then we just trashed them. In the mid-20th century, we turned away from our rivers."

After Kuralt's death, Wodder enlisted Stephen Ambrose, who spurred the effort for several years, making huge contributions in money and visibility. In her office in Washington, D.C., is a photo of Ambrose explaining things to Vice President Dick Cheney—or trying to.

Ambrose would become a nationally heard voice on the Missouri.

"For more than 25 years, the Missouri River has been like a member of my family," he wrote in an op-ed piece appearing in *The Oregonian* in February 2000. "Whether we were backpacking the Lolo Trail in Idaho, camping at Lemhi Pass on the Montana border or canoeing through one of many thunderstorms, the Missouri River has brought my wife, children and me together in more ways than I can measure."

Ambrose helped draw in other voices: commercial fishermen, river towns needing a new economic identity, and people wondering if there's something wrong with a management system that has given the Missouri four 100-year floods in eight years.

"The Missouri River could be as much of an economic engine for tourism as the Rocky Mountains and the oceans are to those states," said Wodder in 2002. "What the bicentennial brings to us is a stage to tell the story of what the rivers were like 200 years ago, and what we can do now."

American Rivers has taken that opportunity and raised the political profile of the rivers that the Corps of Discovery traveled. Riding the bicentennial, it has gone beyond its Beltway lobbyist identity to get in touch with people around the country, rallied supporters to contact congressmen, and used Lewis and Clark's journals to demonstrate the changes in the rivers and amplify its call for renewal. But it has also taken serious hits, starting with the loss of one of its major resources—Ambrose himself, from cancer.

"If we hadn't lost Steve in the fall of 2002," said Wodder, "we would have gotten a lot more attention to the conservation message than we got."

Another setback was the defeat in 2004 of Senate Minority Leader Tom Daschle (D-S.D.), who was both an assertive challenger of the Bush administration's environmental policy and an active spokesman for the river interests of Upper Missouri states. Daschle had received American Rivers' first Lewis and Clark Award at the grand opening of the traveling exhibit.

"No longer having Tom Daschle in the Senate is a blow," admitted Wodder. Other senators from the area hear from and reflect their constituents' views about the river, she said, but "frankly, right now I don't know where the leadership is going to come from."

Overall, the effort hasn't done much better in the judicial than in the executive and legislative branches.

In November 2002, American Rivers, joined by the National Wildlife Federation, the Izaak Walton League, and three state wildlife federations, sued the Army Corps of Engineers over its management of the Missouri. Other suits followed, and in August 2003 a federal judge ordered the Corps to reduce its downriver flow for one week, to balance interests and help protect some species. But in June 2004, another judge refused to order the Corps to change its overall policies, expressing confidence that by 2006 the agency would overhaul its policies on its own.

American Rivers retired to plan its appeals for the following spring. On the Missouri, fall marks the end of the spawning, tourism, and litigation seasons. But the decisions of 2005 were no more encouraging.

"On the Missouri, we've come up against a brick wall of the Corps of Engineers not being willing to make the kind of changes so clearly needed for the first half of the 21st century," mourned Wodder. "There has been a huge lost opportunity."

What's also been missing in the West for years is a truly rainy season, a year that would provide water levels to float Missouri navigation, North Dakota recreation, Montana agriculture, and Columbia-Snake salmon.

"When there is lots of water, people are happy," said Paul Johnston of the Army Corps of Engineers in Omaha in 2003. "When there isn't, people get their toes stepped on. The biggest problem today is drought. Parts of Montana are in their fifth, maybe sixth year of drought."

Two years later, in 2005, the count was higher. An extreme drought covered the country's entire northwest corner, from Montana west, crunching the lands where both the Missouri and the Snake rose. The bicentennial approached with terrific weather for tourists but low liquid levels for water-skiers and salmon.

The policy climate was no more encouraging.

"Thank God," said Wodder, "that salmon are as strong as they are, and maybe they'll survive the human stupidity they're facing now."

In December 2004, outgoing Washington Governor Gary Locke set a goal of managing the Columbia for a massive increase in salmon stocks. But the Bush administration showed little interest—although Judge Redden's June 2005 decision encouraged environmentalists. And American Rivers insists that the bicentennial connection has moved its agenda, especially the traveling exhibition.

"We're continuing to try to shape public opinion to recognize that in the 21st century, there are values that come out of healthy river values," says Wodder. "It maybe has not worked out to the greatest extent, but I'm reasonably happy. Without the bicentennial, it wouldn't have happened."

The man is crying. One of the great stereotypes of the American Indian, setting off eye-rolling exasperation and angry snorts among tribal members, is the Tonto image of cigar-store stoicism—Indians get very emotional about being called unemotional—but this Mandan-Hidatsa is clearly crying. And it's not the single tear rolling down the cheek of the old anti-littering TV spot, but a bursting sob, racking his body and crumpling his face.

Most of the people around him seem not to notice.

He's the central figure in a giant photograph in the American Rivers traveling exhibit—and maybe the central figure of the exhibit. The picture shows the final signing of the agreement—which is probably the wrong word—to build the Garrison Dam in North Dakota, flooding the mid-20th-century homeland of the Mandan, Hidatsa, and Arikara tribes and moving them 200 miles up the Missouri.

By himself, the figure carries the message of how much the Missouri has been changed, and at what cost.

Since 2001, the exhibit has been traveling Lewis and Clark country, up and down the Missouri, in and out of the Pacific Northwest, and back in again, swooping back to Charlottesville and Louisville.

No surroundings—from a Virginia basketball court to an Omaha zoo to a Montana mall to Seattle's Pacific Science Center—have ever eased the crying Mandan-Hidatsas' pain, and the number seeing him and the rest of the exhibit will total well over a million.

The exhibit, designed to recapitulate the expedition's trip west along the major river systems, is built around 12 large panels, one for each part of the journey. It features a re-created prow from the keelboat—including a cannon—oversized maps and charts, and four hours of interactive computer chatting. Through the co-sponsorship of the History Channel, viewers can see an endless tape loop of an interview with Stephen Ambrose—still speaking for the Missouri years after his death.

The exhibit is also co-sponsored by the Army Corps of Engineers, which made American Rivers' lawsuit against the Corps neither more friendly nor less resentful.

For about two hours—depending on how much interactivity you're into or how much History Channel you've already gotten at home—visitors can see river systems they can no longer see anywhere else. They can hear voices from the past and present, talking about the rivers and their meaning.

And they can see an unknown man, probably long dead, weeping as though his heart would break for something that will never come again.

The exhibit's battle cry, "a Missouri River Lewis and Clark would recognize," may be out of reach. But there is a vision—maybe the better word is crossing—toward rivers managed to be more accessible, more protective of species, and more inviting toward people and less of the assumption that a river is just another transportation system to be operated like an oddly wet cloverleaf intersection.

And there are places, along the trail, where the vision is taking shape.

Or, maybe, flowing.

Celilo would be the hardest one. Anyone who knew anything about the history of the Columbia River could figure that.

For centuries, maybe for longer, tribes had gathered at Celilo Falls—a roaring cataract at a place now about 100 miles east of Portland—for fishing and trade. Groups and families had gathered around the scaffoldings that fishermen built alongside the falls, a Columbia pilgrimage point.

The natural impact was powerful. Lewis and Clark, who in their eagerness to get to the Pacific ran some of the Columbia's more dangerous waterfalls, portaged around Celilo. For 150 years after the Corps of Discovery passed, the falls remained a center for the tribes as the world changed around them. Then, in the 1950s, the building of The Dalles Dam flooded Celilo, putting the historic falls under 50 feet of water. Fifty years later, the tribal scars are still on the surface.

So when the Confluence Project, in Vancouver, Washington, began imagining the Lewis and Clark bicentennial's most powerful statement on the Columbia River, the challenge of Celilo would protrude like a stone in a shoe.

In May 1999, Antone Minthorn, chairman of the board of trustees of the Confederated Tribes of the Umatilla Indian Reservation, watched a PBS documentary on Maya Lin, designer of the Vietnam Veterans Memorial in Washington, D.C.—and immediately concluded he had found the person to tell the story of the Columbia and its tribes.

The idea also occurred, almost simultaneously, to the Friends of Lewis and Clark of Pacific County, on the Columbia's southwest shore, and Jane Jacobsen, a Vancouver, Washington, public-affairs organizer—and perhaps the only person in the Northwest to have both a degree in public speaking and theatre from the University of Arkansas and a certificate of excellence from the Zurich Folk Art Institute.

When Jacobsen found on the Web a quote of Lin wondering what the land had been like before Lewis and Clark passed, the sense of possibility compounded. It took six months for all the groups to write the letter inviting her and almost another year for Lin to accept. In May 2001, representatives of the tribes and the other groups visited her New York studio to talk about ideas.

When Celilo came up, things got very quiet.

Over the next four years, the Confluence Project grew into a $22 million effort—with federal, state, local, and private funding—to create sites at seven locations along the Columbia-Snake corridor, from Clarkston, Washington, on the Idaho state line to Cape Disappointment on the Pacific Ocean. Each installation would touch on the Lewis and Clark expedition, but also on what it found.

"Confluence for us is a multilayered meaning," said Jacobsen. "It's not just the river, it's the people, time, the economy, ways of looking at life. Our story, this great Columbia River story, the 10,000-year story of the river, has not been told."

But the story was always there, just covered over, like Celilo Falls.

Lin's plans for the various locations developed slowly over time, through visits, consultations with local residents, and redesigns. In December 2004, she came out to ponder the Clarkston site, a slight urban figure among the rural-built Nez Perce elders. The site picked was a place of tribal vision quests, and Lin imagined an amphitheater of basalt steps, telling the story of the Nez Perce, and a viewing dock over the Snake.

At the other end of the project, where the Columbia finds the sea, a platform will cantilever over the Columbia, with a river path leading to a 12-foot fish-cleaning station marked with the story of the Chinook and a trail up the hill carrying the names of all the tribes met by the expedition. The Cape Disappointment project will be the first site completed.

Celilo will be the last.

The original idea was for a wind tunnel that re-created the sound of the falls; but a wind tunnel to do that would soar upward, and Lin was determined not to set up the tallest element in the neighborhood. The remaining options were vague, but one principle was decided: the installation would be about loss.

It's not the entire story of the Columbia over the last 200 years and the last 100 centuries, but it's part of it. Along with survival—of the tribes depicted along the way and of the terns and herons of the bird-watching blind to be designed on the Sandy River delta—it is a theme to shape the river's next 200 years.

"If the timing is right," said Lin in March 2005, "it's the beginning of telling the story of the river."

What makes St. Louis important is the rivers," said Peter Sortino, president of the civic group St. Louis 2004. "The problem is, you can't get to the rivers."

St. Louis 2004 was formed to mark the bicentennials of Lewis and Clark and the Louisiana Purchase and the centennial of the 1904 World's Fair and Olympics. City leaders decided St. Louis needed major urban projects for the occasion—and after a number of metropolitan-area town-hall meetings, reconnecting to the rivers floated to the top.

In 2000, voters in St. Louis, two suburban Missouri counties, and two suburban Illinois counties created the Metropolitan Parks and Recreation District, funded by an extra tenth of a cent on the sales tax. The new district hired Minneapolis parks director David Fisher and began to devise a plan to improve access to the rivers with parks, bike trails, and a downtown stair-step to the Mississippi.

The district is also raising awareness of how people connect to the rivers—and what they should do about it.

"Everybody belongs to a watershed," Fisher says. "What you put in your drain will end up in one of the rivers."

In 2003, while seeking more ideas for river connections, the district changed its name to the less bureaucratic, more lyrical Great Rivers Greenway.

"What the bicentennial has recalled to us is how we've turned our back on the rivers," Fisher says. "Any celebration that celebrates anything that happened on the rivers is a way to recall why we're here."

The rivers are also why people are in Kansas City, Sioux City, the Dakotas, Montana, and the Pacific Northwest—and why Lewis and Clark traveled through all of them.

Americans have generally had strong feelings—which is not the same as thoughtful plans—about their rivers, the reasons many of us are where we are. An occasion like the Lewis and Clark bicentennial, commemorating a trek that covered a lot of ground but mostly advanced on water, brings our rivers to a high tide of attention.

Doug Bereuter served as congressman for the eastern end of Nebraska—with a state boundary formed by the Missouri—for 13 terms through 2004. He was a founder of the Lewis and Clark Caucus and one of the House members most involved with the bicentennial. The congressman's office often handed out a list of Bereuter's Lewis and Clark legislative achievements, including the extremely posthumous promotion of William Clark to captain. But Bereuter was particularly interested in where the trail touched the Missouri.

"I think a lot of communities have turned their back on the river," explained Bereuter early on. "This has a claim of economic potential. I wanted this to build something that remains afterward."

He even started with an idea on something to build on: "There's a stretch of the river around Sioux City that does look very much like what Lewis and Clark saw."

In drawing a moral from the story of Lewis and Clark, one place to start is just where Thomas Jefferson and Meriwether Lewis started, a theme that shines along 2,400 miles of the Missouri and 1,000 miles of the Columbia system, like sunlight on the current:

A little imagination about rivers can change everything.

Profile

Maya Lin

Maya Lin draws as she talks, not so much to illustrate to her listeners as to connect what she's talking about to what she's saying. As she talks about a basalt slab shaped as a fish-cleaning table, about cedar logs set to mark a location, the images emerge on the piece of paper under her fingers, and it becomes a three-way conversation: Lin and the lines and the listener.

"The thing about cedars is, they grow straight," she explains as she draws long cylinders, "and if you're not careful, you'll get things looking like telephone poles."

As a senior at Yale, Lin won the design contest for the Vietnam Memorial on the Washington Mall, and the world changed. Her image of a black marble "V" sunk into the ground, inscribed with the names of 58,000 U.S. war dead in Vietnam, stirred fury among veterans' groups. One federal arts official recalled hearings where hundreds testified to denounce the idea as unpatriotic and disrespectful. But when the memorial opened, the effect was immediate. Now, 10,000 visitors a day make the pilgrimage to the wall, and its black granite reflects back flowers, handwritten notes, and personal mementoes left at the foot of each panel, closest to the name that drew the visit.

Early in her 20s, Lin became a legend—although, even as she continued to produce prominent installations, she remained a low-profile legend whose conversation frequently features the word "reticent."

On a spring day in 2005, Lin was in Clarkston, Washington, for a Nez Perce blessing of one site in her current and largest effort—the Confluence Project, seven installations along the Columbia and Snake rivers to mark the Lewis and Clark bicentennial. She sat at a hotel breakfast table, with the bare brown-green hills of Idaho rising past the Snake in the background, and explained: "I go crazy if I think of it as seven artworks. To me, it's one artwork, and one river."

Still in varying conceptual stages in 2005, the Confluence Project is one artwork intended to express many messages. Where the Sandy River flows into the Columbia, Lin sees an elevated duck blind, with information evoking all the new-to-science species the Corps of Discovery found on its trip—and the status of those species today. There will be a boat launch, at a place where the Corps entered the Columbia, and a compass showing the former homelands of the tribes of the region and how many remain. Cape Disappointment, where the Columbia and the Corps reach the Pacific, would be the first project completed, in time for the November 2005 bicentennial Signature Event at the mouth of the Columbia.

As in the Vietnam Memorial and Lin's other works, the connection is not dictated, but open, lying there for the traveler or boater to bring his own recognition to it. "You may or may not make a connection," said Lin. "I can't do anything more than that."

While the bicentennial is the theme and the occasion for the project, on several of the sites the explorers might be, as they were in 1805 and 1806, just passing through. Each site would bear a Lewis and Clark inscription, but the projects wouldn't strain for connection between the expedition and the land or between the Corps and the tribes it encountered. "At certain points they intersected," said Lin. "But oftentimes, it's not about meeting, but about being adjacent and having little in common."

What does bring everything together for Lin are the materials involved. Her father was a ceramicist and dean of the School of Art at Ohio University, and her absorption with what she works with spills off the paper she draws on.

"Yesterday I went to see the basalt quarry," she said, her eyes looking at something far from the breakfast table. "As an artist, I was in heaven. I'm going for something that's the perfect shape, and I'm really going to find it. It's like what [Japanese-American sculptor Isamu] Noguchi would do, finding the life of the rock."

Peter Attila Anrushi, a Portland stoneworker chosen to shape the slab chosen, joined her at the quarry, where he saw "her sense of awe at what nature was conveying."

On all seven sites, the fundamental element is the land itself, with its different angles and different messages and, always, the river that connects it. By 2005, Lin's major projects across the country had not focused on a river, but they had dipped deeply into water, its power to shape and its capacity to cleanse. Her *Timetable* at Stanford and the *Women's Table* at Yale, marking women's presence at the university, are water tables, and in her Civil Rights Memorial in Montgomery, Alabama, water flows over the words of Martin Luther King, Jr.: "We are not satisfied and we will not be satisfied until justice rolls down like waters and righteousness like a mighty stream."

Throughout the West, there is no mightier stream than the Columbia River, flowing through the Northwest's territory and its history.

The Confluence Project would be the Northwest's most dramatic bi-centennial outcome, stretching from the Pacific to Idaho, the creation of a commemorative superstar. It is a powerful symbol for the region's tribes; and although Lin declared, "I have a real reticence for seeing what I do in terms of tourism," local leaders along the rivers didn't.

As one county official declared happily at the blessing ceremony, "It's going to bring thousands of people to the area, and we're going to be proud to show them a good time."

Lin is the force of the Confluence Project, and it's hard to imagine it existing without her. Asked why she said yes to it, she retorted quickly, "I didn't say yes. I said no. Many times."

She didn't, she said, want to be marked as "Memorials by Maya."

Then Lin was called by Washington Governor Gary Locke, a fellow Yalie who she had met and contributed to when he was running to be the first Chinese-American state governor. She agreed to consider the idea, and the Confluence planners brought Nez Perce, Umatilla, and Chinook tribal leaders to meet her.

"I said yes," she said in Clarkston, "when I realized who was asking."

By mid-2005, after years of working on the project, she had been across the state of Washington five times. She explained, "Driving the Palouse"—the high, dry, wheat country of eastern Washington—"has got to be one of my most favorite things to do."

Besides, after the Vietnam Memorial, the Civil Rights Memorial, and the *Women's Table*, the Confluence Project fit another priority.

"I am an incredibly committed environmentalist," said Lin. "This isn't about making us go back to pristine land, but about how we treat the land, and how we try to see the land. I go to cities and I don't notice buildings the way I notice landscapes."

Lin is a slight, quiet figure, who often seemed even more so next to elaborately dressed, instinctively ceremonial tribal elders. But her connection was quick and deep. Among other places, it got everybody to the easternmost site, a natural indentation on a hill on an island in the Snake River.

The original plan, supported by local businessmen, envisioned this Confluence site in downtown Clarkston, and Lin came to meet the Nez Perce elders about it. On that visit, Wilfred Scott, known universally as Scotty, later recalled feelingly, "This young lady saw something in all of our hearts and minds, that we didn't think it was in the right place."

And, as it so often seems to with Lin, there was also a Vietnam connection. Tribal people serve heavily in the military, and honors for veterans are often at the center of tribal events. That morning on the river, Scotty carried an eagle feather and wore tribal symbols and braids, but also a "Vietnam Veteran" baseball cap. Speaking at the ceremony, he said of Lin's Vietnam Memorial, "That memorial may be simple, but that memorial covers the world."

Now, seven miles down the river from Clarkston, the feeling among the 100 people gathered for the blessing—men on one side, women on the other—was that the project had found its right location. A highway runs down on one side and a railroad on the other, but on top of the hill it was almost eerily quiet—except for sudden bursts of bird screechings. The surrounding hillsides hold a handful of houses, but mostly long stretches of vertical greenery and basalt.

"I call it the sky bowl," said Lin. "It's the only site that places you in the river, where you can get an idea of what it might have been like for Lewis and Clark to look up."

Up on top of a hill, in Chief Timothy Park on an island in the Snake River, listeners heard not only the voices of today, or even the voices of Lewis and Clark, but voices from all the years in between.

Antone Minthorn, chairman of the Confluence board, wore a navy Umatilla reservation sweatshirt reading "Lovin' Life on the Rez." He recalled the 1855 tribal treaty that ceded 6.4 million acres of northeast Oregon and southeast Washington to the United States. During the negotiations, said Minthorn, a leader named Young Chief asked the American officers, "What would the land say if it knew what we knew doing?"

That voice still needs to be heard, explained Minthorn, and he continued with certainty, "Maya's going to do that. The land is going to speak to her, and she's going to interpret. She's got the gift to do that."

Across 200 years and the full width of the Northwest and seven different sites, there is a lot to hear.

Five

The New West, with Postcards

The 13-year-old girl, elaborately arranged in gingham, bonnet, and petticoats, came toiling up the slope from the Missouri River, only to hear a sibling urge her to move faster. Swiftly, the 21st-century teenager came bursting out of the 19th-century demeanor: "You're not the one wearing four layers, are you?"

No, but a lot of other people were.

In May 2004, the Lewis and Clark bicentennial set off up the Missouri River, from the same riverbank where the Corps of Discovery departed 200 years before. The village hosted one of the bicentennial's Signature Events, with 75,000 visitors one weekend, a total twice that, and repeated parades complete with the St. Charles Fife and Drum Corps—a precision unit modeled on an 1800 U.S. Army corps, if the corps had been made up of adolescents and a co-ed.

The casting off from St. Charles achieved an even more perfect symmetry: a re-created expedition cast off from a re-created village.

"The habitants of the old French village are role-playing today," read the signs all over St. Charles' historic section, warning visitors before they came across a blacksmith pounding on iron, or a farmer patting an ox, or a barefoot dairywoman trying to sell tourists some eggs. "It is 1804."

Actually, according to the visitors' digital watches, it wasn't. But St. Charles reflected a strong and increasingly alluring tourism theme central to the bicentennial, from Jeffersonian dinners to overnights in Sioux tepees to horseback tours in Idaho to the planned salt trail from Fort Clatsop to the ocean—the eagerness not only to learn history but also to somehow experience it.

The idea is that just as you can visit San Francisco or London, you can visit 1804.

It is one measure of what people sought in the bicentennial that so many want to make that trip. The travel industry expression is "heritage tourism," and whether you think of it as retirees setting out in Winnebagos to find their roots or Germans looking for the Wild West they read about in Karl May (the German Zane Grey), it moves bodies—often into unexpected places. The past, it turns out, isn't dead. It's a tourist attraction.

For the Lewis and Clark bicentennial, the past's tourist attraction surged sharply with Stephen Ambrose's book and Ken Burns' PBS documentary, both appealing to just the relatively upscale heritage tourism market that local planners hungered after. As Paul Lloyd-Davies of the Lewis and Clark Interpretive Center in Great Falls—with a parking lot full of license plates running east to New England and south to North Carolina—explained about his visitors, "Most of them say they read *Undaunted Courage* and got interested."

A few hundred yards up the riverbank from the petticoated teen-ager in St. Charles, Nik Yeager of Palmyra, Missouri, considered what he was doing there. He began thoughtfully, "I'm a kind of admirer of the Corps of Discovery," before his wife Teresa interrupted, "He's read every book ever written on it."

The next day, as the re-enacting boats prepared to set off up the Missouri, Scott Pioske, a truck line dispatcher, explained why he and several friends have driven down from Fairfax, Minnesota, to see it—and why, before this, they went to the Louisville event and expected to be heading out to the Dakotas.

"It's a unique journey in history," he said about the expedition. The bicentennial is "something you can only do once. It's a nice way to relive it."

Towns across the entire trail were eager to help him try.

Any of the many western chambers of commerce hunting tourists would consider Marietta Castle a particularly fine specimen. The summer before the re-enactment began, Castle, an educational consultant from Rock Island, Illinois, was collecting her purchases in the gift shop of Fort Union, on the western edge of North Dakota, thoroughly enjoying her 10th day on the Lewis and Clark Trail.

Castle knew exactly what had sent her out into the relative wilderness—a fascination with the Missouri and a fascination with the story.

"We kept reading more," she recalled, "and just said, we've got to see the trail."

That draw is what a lot of places like North Dakota were looking to build on in the 21st century. It was a measure of the economic condition of so many places along the trail that so many places saw the bicentennial not as part of their past but as a piece of their future. The Lewis and Clark expedition—once the area's opening—was seen as its opportunity.

Kansas, one of the nation's least tourist-targeted states—at least since the end of the heyday of the Atchison, Topeka, & Santa Fe—and only a peripheral stop-by for the expedition, still claimed a piece of a bicentennial Signature Event and dug into a small state tourist budget to advertise its Lewis and Clarkness in *National Geographic.* Even states whose involvement with the expedition predated its actual departure west—such as Pennsylvania and West Virginia—claimed moments in the story that visitors shouldn't miss.

"Many of the areas on the trail, by their nature, could use a shot in the arm economically," admitted Representative Brian Baird, as he watched the bicentennial approach from the Cannon House Office Building.

On the Washington coast, in Baird's district, the expedition first saw the Pacific Ocean—and the current residents have seen their logging and fishing economy collapse.

To Baird, as to many hopeful hosts along the trail, the bicentennial might produce even more than passers-through with cameras and American Express cards. "For 50 percent of the companies that relocate," Baird said enthusiastically and gamely, "the first encounter came through tourism."

By the end of 2004, it seemed clear that the most extravagant projections of bicentennial travel—tourists thronging the trail in buffalo-like herds—were unlikely to happen. Still, the hosts of many of the early events, from Louisville to North Dakota, were pleased by turnout, and the bicentennial still seemed a way to raise the tourism profiles of places not typically high on the recreational radar screen.

Nobody ever won a Super Bowl, looked into the camera, and announced, "I'm going to Chamberlain, South Dakota!"

In 200 years, the West has burned through or overused so many natural resources—furs, buffalo, timber, mining, fishing, grazing—that many parts of the region are almost down to their landscape and their history. By protecting and cultivating both, many westerners hope to develop tourists as the land's new renewable resource.

Along the full length of the trail—and in places hundreds of miles from it—activists and developers were pushing for local economic benefits from the bicentennial. The hopes extend from Louisville, Kentucky, where a new statue of York, Clark's slave, was calculated to build interest in the city's African-American history museum, to Idaho and Montana, where canoe, horseback, and backpacking guides were counting on the event to build wilderness tourism, to Baird's constituents on the Pacific, who have invested in the bicentennial as if it were a reborn wild salmon run.

The idea of running bed-and-breakfasts and posing for photos, of course, is not exactly the classic western self-image—typically, more ranching than brunching, more cattle-driving than catering. To some locals, and some outside observers, the new trail seems hardly straight.

"If one looks for a different, and more reliable, kind of foundation, all roads seem to lead to tourism, to the preservation and publicizing of local and natural and cultural resources, as a permanent attraction for visitors with deep pockets," concedes University of Colorado Professor Patricia Nelson Limerick, a trail boss of the new western historians, before noting, "In tourism's Third World labor arrangements, in its often terrible disparity between rich and poor in places like Aspen, in its various environmental impacts from sewage to air pollution, and in its ongoing vulnerability to the swings of the American economy, tourism may be an unappealing alternative to mining, logging, ranching and farming. But what else is there?"

The original Lewis and Clark expedition was intended to see what was out there. After 200 years, one of the motivations of the bicentennial was to see what else was out there.

The tourism industry, as Limerick notes and as a lot of ocean and ski towns have learned, includes a large number of low-wage jobs, just in the places where out-of-town money shoots up housing and living costs. It is vulnerable not only to overall economic shifts but also to sudden gasoline price spikes and, these days, to the shifting prospects of the terror threat scale. As historian Hal Rothman has argued, western tourism is a "devil's bargain," ultimately vaporizing the local atmosphere and marginalizing much of the local population. But it is also a way to bring outside money into communities increasingly desperate for it. And tourism does generally encourage preserving the local landscape rather than slicing it up and shipping it away.

And while people no longer wear beaver hats, nobody seems likely to stop going on vacation.

At one end of the trail, the re-created village of St. Charles demonstrates how the past can be profitably recycled, with a cobblestoned street full of restaurants, an enthusiastically cooperating local population, dazzling re-creations of Lewis and Clark's boats—often, admittedly, away on business during the bicentennial itself—and major metropolitan areas nearby.

At the other end, at the mouth of the Columbia River, the Oregon town of Astoria—the oldest American town west of the Rockies, founded just a few years after Lewis and Clark spent the winter just over the hill—looked to the bicentennial as part of its recovery from the disappearance of dozens of canneries that once lined the riverfront.

"In the back of everyone's mind about taking a risk," explained Astoria developer Chester Trabucco in late 2003, "if there ever was a good time, this is it. Because of that, things are popping up all over the place."

Trabucco was speaking in the lobby of his newly renovated Hotel Elliott, originally built to house river pilots and now retargeted for tourists. At the time, offered in each room—not quite displacing the Gideon Bible but certainly more prominently displayed—was a copy of writer Rex Ziak's book on Lewis and Clark's wanderings in the area, *In Full View*.

It's Astoria's version of the St. Charles Fife and Drum Corps.

In between the two river cities, a huge stretch of the trail is in Montana—where, its promoters point out, Lewis and Clark spent more nights than anywhere else. Since then, Montana has become iconically western, the Big Sky Country, the "Last, Best Place," with its mountains, rivers, and plains as familiar a movie backdrop as the back lot New York street. Montana, from ranches to grizzlies, is the classic image of the American West—and a river runs through it.

Actually, two key Lewis and Clark rivers run through it—the Missouri and the Yellowstone.

But in the last decades of the 20th century, Montana became the state of Big Sky and small wages. In a state that once featured the "Richest Hill on Earth" in Butte, the mines played out, and agriculture, already reeling, wilted under a multiyear drought. In November 2004, when Montana parted a red sea by electing a Democratic governor and legislature, the state party's executive director was clear on the motivation: "We ran on things like the fact that we lead the nation in percentage of households where people have to work two jobs, and we're at the bottom for average wages."

Montana's recent growth industry has been its role as a playground for outsiders, as wealthy wanderers such as Ted Turner amassed large empires of ranchland. Tourism became Montana's second-largest industry—and a big part of that was heritage tourism.

Understandably, the state got deeply into bicentennial planning, with Travel Montana putting $200,000 a year into Lewis and Clark efforts—a lot of money for Montana. So the state's program urging battered ranchers and farmers to preserve their trails and consider opening bed-and-breakfasts went forth, under the title "Undaunted Stewardship."

Get it? Montana hoped to.

Lewis and Clark—for all their vast exploration, tourism trend-setting, and massive souvenir acquisition—were never greeted by a brass band. But this afternoon in late May 2003, the first Lewis and Clark Explorer Train, chugging into Astoria from Portland on rails that had almost forgotten their purpose, was greeted by a dozen tootling Astorians, a barbecued chicken lunch, and a banner the size of a Lewis and Clark keelboat.

And the passengers weren't even carrying warm wishes from Thomas Jefferson. All they brought was the prospect that more of them would follow.

For almost two centuries, Astoria lived fat off the land and sea. The wealth started with trapping sea otters and shipping the pelts to China. It grew to a time when giant logs waited in the river for shipping to Japan, when 38 fish canneries lined the docks and Astoria was the international headquarters of Bumble Bee fishpackers. Today, train passengers can see the naked river pilings sitting where canneries and fish-net barns used to stand, and no major new employers have swept in to replace them.

Now, Astoria is turning from timber and tuna to tourism—and raising a crop of tourists requires a whole different attitude toward the local lands and waters.

The bicentennial has forced the question, says Steve Forrester, editor and publisher of *The Daily Astorian*, but for years there has been "a subliminal question that there's something not good enough about tourism. It's not fishing, it's not lumber, it's not manhood."

But it's a future—and one based solidly on Astoria's past.

Astoria's bicentennial strategies would look familiar to Great Falls, Montana, and to waning Dakota farm towns. But because of the drama of its section of the saga ("Ocian in view!") and the nearness of the ocean and of a major city (Portland), Astoria may have the greatest heritage tourism potential between the Pacific Ocean and St. Louis.

And as the bicentennial approached, Astorians didn't want to miss the train.

Although they were unquestionably the first American tourists to spend a season in the area, Lewis and Clark would not have recommended it to vacationing friends. During their winter at Fort Clatsop—now just a new shuttle-bus ride from downtown Astoria—they complained constantly about the rain. Clark once sniped that he didn't see why the ocean was called Pacific, because it never gave him a peaceful day. Wrote geographer John Logan Allen about the explorers' bleak, boring winter—in language recognizable to anyone who's ever spent a winter in Oregon—"The West was not golden, but gray."

Still, five years after Lewis and Clark's eager departure, a U.S. fur-trading settlement stood at Astoria, spurred by their reporting. "Astoria," wrote historian and writer Bernard DeVoto, "followed from the expedition of Lewis and Clark as the flight of an arrow follows the release of the bowstring." Thomas Jefferson decided that his Louisiana Purchase included Oregon and called Astoria "the germ of a great, free and independent empire carrying all U.S. hopes west of the Rockies." Astoria became the symbol of American imperial ambition until the Oregon Country became officially American in 1846.

For more than a century afterward, Astoria reigned over the mouth of the Columbia. Its wealth was reflected in the elaborate Victorian houses that still cling to the hills overlooking the harbor. Millions of salmon a year went through the canneries, and the industry drew thousands of Swedes and Finns—less sensitive to overcast skies than two explorers from warm Virginia.

Similar patterns could be traced anywhere along the trail, from Irish miners in Montana to German wheat farmers in the Dakotas to St. Louis Italians and African Americans, serving the endless trains that held it all together. The West's natural richness was a bounty reaching around the world.

Then, in the last third of the 20th century, it changed.

Willis Van Dusen's family has been in Astoria since 1843. His grandfather and father were on the city council, his uncle was president of Bumble Bee, and, as the bicentennial approached, he was in his fourth term as mayor. (For his last re-election, a friend put out signs: "Vote for Willis: Four more years won't kill us.") As he talked about his city, Van Dusen was having a good day—his Harley-Davidson had just been fixed and repainted—but as an Astoria leader, he'd seen a lot of bad days.

As the canneries and timber dwindled, he recalled, local leaders "tried to hit the home run, bringing in a big aluminum works or a coastal shopping center. I've seen more beautiful drawings than you can imagine."

Finally, it seemed that something had come off the paper.

"I thought tourism would never be a player in Astoria," Van Dusen said, but "the Lewis and Clark bicentennial is so big they're going to come whether we build it or not."

To Van Dusen, the bicentennial would not only bring thousands of visitors to Astoria—visitors he hoped will return in more leisurely times—but might help address the city's key problem: transportation. Horizon Air, the city's only commercial air connection, had cleared out a few years earlier, and he hoped a bicentennial wave might bring it back.

Then there was the train.

Astoria hadn't had regular rail service to Portland for decades. Even the four-day-a-week, summer-only Lewis and Clark Explorer Train, kicking off in the summer of 2003, stirred gauzy local thoughts of a return of freight service, reopening possibilities for Tongue Point, a manufacturing area in constant quest of a manufacturer.

The second and final summers of the train, in 2004 and 2005, didn't have quite the every-seat-sold cachet of the first. Still, business was strong, and passengers could ride a few feet from the Columbia while consuming Smoke Salmon Newberg en Croute from an Astoria restaurant.

Out of one side of the train, riders could look out at the empty river pilings. Out of the other, they could look up the hill at an earlier attempt to capitalize on the town's history, the 1926 Astoria Column, with its circular mural depicting the tribal landscape, the arrival of Lewis and Clark, and the development of the fur trade. The tower, restored and refurbished in recent years, evokes both the original West and the legendary version—and now looks down on the effort to create a new one.

Even Fort Clatsop itself—or at least the National Park Service's 1950s re-created version—was made more hospitable for tourists, although one still can't imagine Lewis or Clark being eager to return. For the bicentennial, after major heavy lifting by congressmen and senators from both states, the site was expanded, a new trail from the fort to the ocean laid out, and Fort Clatsop itself combined with three nearby Washington expedition sites into the new Lewis and Clark National Historical Park, the first place where the Park Service shares management with two different states.

Oregon and Washington may squabble over the claim to the end of the trail, but they seem willing to share the tourist business.

In Washington, with guidance from Rex Ziak and others, the Long Beach Peninsula has set up an eight-mile Lewis and Clark stretch along its beach, including the place where Clark first saw the ocean. The walk features a whale skeleton—marking a vividly described discovery by the Corps—and an obelisk and compass, a plaque of Jefferson's letter to Lewis, a patch of old-growth Sitka spruce, a whale skeleton, and bronze sculptures of a sturgeon, a condor, and a windswept evergreen with Clark's initials carved in it.

They also have a poster, a videocassette, the site of one of the eagerly anticipated Maya Lin Confluence Project installations, an emerging schedule to mark the 18 days in November 1805 that the expedition spent in the area, and a hope for an enduring impact on their tourist appeal.

Once a place of family cabins with sinks outside for cleaning fish, the Long Beach peninsula has been a tourist destination for 100 years. Now, there are not many fish, but with Lewis and Clark, the peninsula figures it will have something not every beach town has. Declared Nabiel Shawa—then a Long Beach city official and the chair of the state advisory board, now city administrator of Washougal, Washington—"We've got a monopoly on this."

And although everyone on either side of the Columbia had a different guess about how many tourists the bicentennial will bring—100,000 a year? a million over three years?—some people hoped for a special harvest on the tide.

"The Lewis and Clark traveler is going to be more highly educated and more affluent," forecasted the *Astorian*'s Steve Forrester. "A large percentage of business relocation happens when a business owner goes somewhere on a trip." By keelboat or otherwise.

In Astoria, you got the feeling that nobody's waited this eagerly for Lewis and Clark since Thomas Jefferson.

The tourist boat noses through the Missouri River, and around each bend is another sheer wall of rock and trees, with bursts of wildflower colors and birds flying over the cliffs—but no easy pathway west toward the sunset and the Pacific. With the horizon free of cars and transmission towers, you can peer across the helm of the boat and feel just a bit of what must have struck Lewis and Clark as they came through this passage and approached the Rocky Mountains:

This could be more complicated than we thought. And also more stunning.

"This evening we entered much the most remarkable clifts that we have yet seen," Meriwether Lewis wrote in his journal in July 1805 about this stretch of the river. ". . . Every object here wears a dark and gloomy aspect. the tow[er]ing and projecting rocks in many places seem ready to tumble on us. the river appears to have forced it's way through this immence body of solid rock for the distance of 5¾ Miles and where it makes it's exit below has thrown on either side vast columns of rocks mountains high. . . . From the singular appearance of this place I called it the gates of the rocky mountains."

Montana has always made an impression on tourists.

Today's travelers, such as the ones on the summer boat ride through the Gates of the Mountains—just outside Helena, three rocky miles down from Interstate 15—are vital to the economy of this state, which hopes urgently that the Lewis and Clark bicentennial will bring in more of them.

As the Corps of Discovery discovered—coming and going—Montana is a vast place, stretching across the top of the West, big enough to have several different economies. The eastern part is Great Plains, wheat farming, and ranching, and the western part is Rocky Mountains and ranching, with major tribal reservations on both sides. Large mineral deposits, notably copper, made mining and miners a prominent part of the mix and sent Montana copper magnates to the U.S. Senate.

Much of it has now faded, as mining has dropped away to less than 10 percent of the economy. Eastern Montana has experienced the decline and depopulation of the rest of the Plains, and the mountainous western reaches have become increasingly dependent on tourism. After the 1990 census, Montana lost one of its two U.S. House seats, and long-term drought has punished its agriculture since the late 1990s. Now, Montana, the state of small cities and smaller towns, badly needs to make its economy bigger.

Montana's economic realities helped drive the state's investment in the Lewis and Clark bicentennial, to try to maximize its position as the place where the Corps followed the Missouri to its source, encountered the Gates of the Mountains, and—on the way back—split up to explore more territory. Like the Corps of Discovery itself, Montanans see the stakes as high.

Not only can Montana claim that the expedition spent more nights there than anyplace else, it also could have vastly more "Lewis and Clark slept here" sites than any other state. (Except, of course, for the difficulty in finding the exact places where Lewis and Clark slept—eased a little bit by the enduring presence of mercury in the soil from their venereal disease treatments.). In every other trail state, the expedition followed pretty much the same route coming and going, but Montana has three different Lewis and Clark trails—one on the way west and two different ones coming back, as the captains split up to try to find an easier route than the original.

For the bicentennial, vast stretches of a vast state qualified as tourist territory, and Montana worked hard to maximize its possibilities. Along with two of the bicentennial's 15 Signature Events, northeast Montana added its own Signature Event—Lewis and Clark at the Confluence—marking the 200th anniversary of the expedition's entry into Montana.

Montana devised a second Signature Event—Lewis and Clark in the Rockies—for the western part of the state as well as two additional tribal-themed events. The state had been promoting its role in the bicentennial for five years, in magazine ads, cable TV spots, and its own Web sites.

"I think the greatest thing for all of this, for local areas of the entire state," said Betty Stone, in her Betty Boop-themed office at the Cottonwood Inn in Glasgow, in Montana's northeast, "is that we're going to have a legacy of additional tourist opportunities, and educational opportunities for people who live there."

To Stone, who served on the state bicentennial commission, it would help Montana "get some infrastructure in place years after the bicentennial is over."

Northeast Montana might not be the first place you would think of as a tourist attraction. There's the massive Fort Peck Dam, which does create a huge recreational lake, and now there's a museum to hold recently discovered dinosaur bones. But the land is flat, the population sparse, and, as the Corps discovered, it's a long way from anywhere—unless your idea of anywhere is Williston, North Dakota.

But it is on the trail, the population and economy are slipping, and the bicentennial is a hope.

Glasgow's investment was nothing like the commitment of Great Falls, close to the center of the state, about where the mountains begin to erupt out of the Plains. Great Falls banked on a huge, 34-day-long Signature Event—the most ambitious of anyplace on the trail—that could mark both the expedition's emergence from the Plains and Great Falls' emergence as a tourism destination. The city, third-largest in the state, already has tourist visibility, with the Charles M. Russell Museum of Western Art, the Lewis and Clark National Historic Trail Interpretive Center, the falls themselves, and—for anyone arriving from the east, as the expedition did—the first decent latte in hundreds of miles.

Now its plans were bigger.

"In Montana, agriculture is our Number One industry, and it's in trouble," mused Janet Medina, vice president of the Great Falls Chamber of Commerce, in 2003, two years before her city's Signature Event. "Tourism is low-impact. They come here, they experience it, they go home.

"I'm not sure how we could have not paid more attention to tourism before. It's an obvious fit. We are positioning ourselves as a tourism city."

After the first round of Signature Events, from Monticello through North Dakota, it seemed that vast numbers of tourists would not be coming after all. In the second week of the Great Falls event, in June 2005, spokesman Jeanne Kelley Pugh assessed it as "fairly well attended, but not what we had hoped for. Early on in the planning stage, the enthusiasm was running away with people."

Still, the event did draw some visitors from around the country and from Asia and Europe. And the bicentennial could still have a significant effect on Montana's positioning.

In her office in Helena—half an hour from Gates of the Mountains and just off the state capitol's main drag, Last Chance Gulch—Betsy Baumgart explained about what Lewis and Clark could bring to the state. Baumgart, heading the Promotion Division of Travel Montana, had been planning Montana's effort for a while and knew just what she was after.

"Heritage tourism is the fastest growing part of the business," Baumgart said, "and cultural tourists are better-educated and higher-income. That's a goal, to get the visitors to spend more. They're high-income, low-impact visitors."

For Montana, tourism seems like an answer—if not necessarily *the* answer—and if the question is heritage tourism, then the state has plenty of heritage to go around. (It has, at this point, rather more heritage than copper and possibly more heritage than agricultural prospects.) Along the Lewis and Clark Trail, Montana has spectacular heritage, places where the Corps of Discovery encountered natural sights such as Gates of the Mountains and the Missouri Breaks, described in the 19th century as never before seen by non-Native people. Montana has legacies of the expedition itself, such as Pompey's Pillar—near Billings, the site of Montana's other Signature Event—where Clark carved his signature, still visible, the only unquestioned mark left by the expedition in the state.

Montana also has a dramatic but more ambiguous heritage, such as the only place where the expedition actually killed Indians, in a confrontation between Lewis and some Blackfeet. A tribal Signature Event in 2006, covering parts of northwest Montana, would provide a Blackfeet name to what is now called, simply, the Fight Site.

Not all Montana Indians, Clint Blackwood admits, were wild about the idea of the bicentennial, of commemorating Lewis and Clark. Still, the state's seven tribes did gather in the Montana Tribal Tourism Alliance, whose head, Dyani Bingham, declared about travel on reservations that "people shouldn't be afraid to drive through, and roll up their windows."

Already a state where tourism is the second largest industry, Montana seems to have a powerful opportunity to maximize its position. Yet, at least some of the feeling on the subject of a tourist future seems wistful.

During his time as a Republican state senator from Missoula, Dale Mahlum worked to strengthen Montana's bicentennial program and looked forward to the growth in tourism—noting that even before the bicentennial, the state annually brought in 10 times its own population in visitors. Among Mahlum's other businesses—thoroughbred horses and hardware—he owned a recreational vehicle park, giving him a sense of who's coming.

"So many people have comfortably retired," he said, in the living room of a Missoula bed-and-breakfast that itself reflects a changing Montana. "One of the things they're going to do is see about their heritage. These are the people we expect to see in our area. You cannot believe how many people travel by RV."

Still, all the new arrivals, all the new business, and all the new taxes don't sweep him entirely away.

"Our heritage is cattle ranching and wheat farms," says Mahlum. "Our heritage was built from the dirt. We'd like to have tourism come up to be with agriculture, but not pass it."

Looking at the Lewis and Clark bicentennial as a tourist occasion—which was, after all, pretty much the identity of the original expedition—can bring up a battalion of connected questions and doubts. But searching the regional economic horizon can also bring you back to Patricia Nelson Limerick's question: "What else is there?"

The economic identity of the West—especially the interior West—has always been to bring in cash from elsewhere, generally by selling whatever was around. (The fact that so little cash actually stayed in the West has always suggested one weakness of the system.) Now, with the West apparently having less and less that is salable in its historic garage sale, it seems just logical that the only way for cash to get to the Plains and the Rockies is for visitors to bring it themselves.

The West has often felt fleeced in the process, back to the time when the West was in the East and the Whiskey Rebellion rose in western Pennsylvania. Lewis and Clark traveled through the new states of Kentucky and Ohio, settled by arrivals still suspicious of the East Coast, and the pattern of suspicion continued through Populism, the Reagan-era Sagebrush Rebellion, and a current crop of resentful western senators who would be unrecognizable to Thomas Jefferson.

The historic extraction economies of the West have often deepened regional antagonisms. The rising new economic presence, tourism, is itself frequently divisive wherever it arises, creating lines between summer people and locals, between islanders and people from away, between people who ski and people who shine ski boots.

But heritage tourism, the target of the Lewis and Clark market, may be different. Aside from the impression that heritage and cultural tourists are particularly well-heeled and thus particularly welcome—whether or not the PBS-watching, Volvo-driving stereotype is true—their kind of tourism has a different core.

Going to visit Fort Mandan or the Great Falls Signature Event, after all, is not like going to Disney World or even the Grand Canyon. Heritage tourism is based not on happenstance of geography but on common values and experience. People who travel to check out a place of local history presumably bring not just larger MasterCard limits but also a more companionable attitude toward the people who actually live in and take pride in the place.

And they bring away not just a sunburn and a souvenir but also a stronger sense of the places they've visited and the kind of people who live there now. Generally, people don't get that experience from visiting Knott's Berry Farm.

Even in smaller numbers than the original overheated projections, the heritage tourists of the Lewis and Clark bicentennial—like the members of the first 1804-1806 expedition—could become not only an economic element but also a nationally unifying element.

Assuming, of course, that they also spent money.

Profile

James Ronda

The summer before anything in the Lewis and Clark bicentennial got started, the summer that marked the 200th anniversary of nothing but Thomas Jefferson looking west from Monticello and wondering what was out there, James Ronda was due to speak at the Joslyn Museum in Omaha to about 250 people.

A thousand showed up. The trail, it seemed, might have its attractions.

James Ronda doesn't look like someone who, nearly two centuries after the expedition, changed our understanding of Lewis and Clark forever. Slight, balding, with a little mustache, he looks like a political cartoonist's image of John Q. Public. But if Stephen Ambrose wrote the book that started everything, Ronda wrote the book that changed everything.

Lewis and Clark Among the Indians, first published in 1984, may have been the first title that actually gave the tribes equal billing with the icons. The first of more than 10 books Ronda has written or edited about the West, it dramatically broadened the way people talked about the expedition—and also who talked about it. Against an impression of a bold expedition fighting through a wilderness, Ronda wrote of a community moving through other communities, noting that Thomas Jefferson "grasped what so often escaped others, that the American West was a crowded wilderness."

In the Corps of Discovery story, *Lewis and Clark Among the Indians* gave considerably more prominent speaking roles to figures such as Black Buffalo and Coboway—and swiftly to Ronda himself. He became the foremost historian of the expedition and, especially after the death of Stephen Ambrose in 2002, the major historical voice of the bicentennial. When President George W. Bush turned down the invitation to keynote the bicentennial's opening at Monticello, Ronda replaced him. As the bicentennial approached, Ronda consulted on museum exhibitions across the country and on documentaries from PBS and the BBC to Disney. Throughout 2004, Ronda spoke 17 times around the country on the meaning of Lewis and Clark—at Signature Events, exhibition openings, and historical societies—encountering many of the expedition's travel troubles plus jet lag.

He fielded questions on everything from where the expedition fits into U.S. history to how many dogs the Corps of Discovery ate—although he couldn't answer that one exactly. At home at the University of Tulsa, he gets e-mail questions almost every day, and tries to answer them all.

To Ronda, it was an opportunity all around, and the questions he got—on the road and in cyberspace—explained the interest level in the bicentennial at this time in western history.

"I think this is one of those moments of redefinition we go through consistently in the West," he said. "Our definitions of the West are constantly changing."

One way definitions change is through shifting attitudes among professors—an evolution reflected in contemporary Lewis and Clark authorities such as Ronda, geographer John Logan Allen, and historian Gary Moulton, editor of the recent multi-volume edition of the Lewis and Clark journals. Ronda's own graduate school experience, at Nebraska in the late 1960s, was shaped by the attitudes of the time: a new sensitivity to civil rights issues, Indians, environmental impacts. It helped him look at Lewis and Clark with different eyes—and listen with different ears.

"When I meet with native people, I don't say very much," said Ronda. "You talk, I'll listen. Americans have a hard time being quiet. I'm a good listener. I was trained by Studs Terkel. Studs knew how to ask one question and then listen."

The range of his conversations also gave Ronda a somewhat less reverential attitude toward the captains—and even toward their journals—than many of the nation's Lewis and Clark enthusiasts. Ronda's viewpoint was expressed in his assessment of Lewis' accounts of the Indians: "He could bring to life a weapon or a skin shirt, but the people who created these objects always seemed just beyond his reach."

To a story that often seems comprised of heroic figures—of bronze images of Lewis and Clark and Sacagawea and, increasingly, York and Lewis' dog Seaman—Ronda brought a less statuesque approach. "If you come to the Lewis and Clark story seeking comfort, go some other place," he told audiences. "Anyone who thinks this is a small story with a handful of actors should look again."

Still, Ronda was pleased with most aspects of the bicentennial, including the parts that wanted nothing to do with complexity—the parts that put pictures on T-shirts and featured banquets with Thomas Jefferson Split Pea Soup. Any major event like the bicentennial, he thought, needs to provide both education and entertainment, and observers experience it all at different levels at different times—just as, he said, people get different things out of *Moby Dick* and *The Scarlet Letter* depending on whether they are adults reading for pleasure or high-school students plowing through an assignment.

The strength of the Lewis and Clark bicentennial was that it drew from both sides, from heroic legend and from the analytic reconsideration—drawing, you might say, from both second grade and second thoughts. The importance of both was clear from two recent historical commemorations that fell as flat as a marked-down baseball cap.

In 1992, the 500th anniversary of the voyage of Christopher Columbus to the New World, noted Ronda, featured little conversation and a lot of confrontation. As he put it, the quincentenary occurred at "a different time in our cultural lives." Its main products were anger and an example that may terrify planners until the 600th anniversary. A few years afterward, Ronda pointed out, the 150th anniversary of the Oregon Trail just didn't catch anybody's interest—despite all the emotional potential of 3,000 surviving trail diaries. Maybe that trail just lacked outsized heroes who could fit on a sweatshirt or a roadside sign.

Of course, there's also something particularly compelling about Lewis and Clark's two-and-a-half-year, 8,000-mile, against-the-odds round trip to the end of the world and back.

"It's a story about a journey, and we are a journeying people," said Ronda. "The journey is one of the fundamentals about us."

The emotional wallop of a trail never before traveled is part of what makes the Lewis and Clark story an inviting piece of what Americans seek in their history—what Ronda calls, quoting Henry James, "the visitable past."

Appropriately, Ronda has a visitable past of his own, carefully preserved in a room in his house.

"I grew up in Chicago in the last days of steam, and the sights and sounds of your childhood are imprinted on you," he explained. "I love trains, just as I love jazz and blues."

The elaborate train set he's built to channel that affection evokes another part of his past—Youngstown, Ohio, where he taught for two decades at Youngstown State University, declining other offers because he had promised his daughter not to move until she finished high school. (After she graduated in 1990, he was recruited by Tulsa to be the H.G. Barnard Professor of Western American History.) But the Youngstown of his layout is a city that predates his own arrival. Ronda's trains steam through the booming steel-mill downtown of 1955, a landscape already departing when Ronda arrived in Youngstown in 1969 and virtually vanished today.

That place exists now only in Ronda's basement—and in his imagination. The idea that places exist not only in reality and on maps but in the memory and expectation of people is central to Ronda's thinking about the geography of the West. It's behind his account of Thomas Jefferson's interest in "the country of the mind out past St. Louis."

The expectation and hope that Jefferson, and two centuries of other Americans, had about the West was so powerful that it often overwhelmed what was actually there—or just ignored it.

Sitting in the Colonnade Club at the University of Virginia, a guest house for distinguished visitors at the center of the campus, Ronda could look up at a literal signpost of a one country of the mind. It's a map of the United States at about the time of Lewis and Clark. On it, Ohio is already a state, Mississippi is still a territory, and west of the Mississippi River the printing swiftly peters out into blankness.

It has been Ronda's argument for 20 years, to an increasingly receptive audience, that the blankness on the early 19th-century map didn't reflect what was really there, that the empty spaces were actually filled by dozens of complex tribal societies. It is a vision of the West of 200 years ago that affects Ronda's view of the 21st-century West and causes him to see the bicentennial from yet another angle.

"If there is an emptiness, perhaps it is today, with fewer plants, fewer animals and a mind-numbing similarity of strip malls," said Ronda, sitting beneath the historical map. "I've been traveling the Lewis and Clark Trail since the 1970s, and I've seen dramatic change. The West is a fragile place. We have this propensity to chew up the landscape."

It's one of the things—including who we are, where we've been, and where we're going—that a bicentennial gives us a chance to reconsider. As Lewis and Clark discovered, a lot can happen over two and half years.

"In a strange and mysterious way," Ronda told the shivering crowd in his January 2003 bicentennial keynote at Monticello, "even across the divide of two centuries, they are us and we are them. . . . If we finish the journey in 2006 being the same people we are now, what William Clark called 'so vast an enterprise' will have failed."

James Ronda knows something about the power of the story.

"Don Jackson [one of the first Lewis and Clark scholars and editor of their letters] told me a long time ago my life would be shaped by Lewis and Clark," he recalled before stepping out in front of Jefferson's back porch—facing, naturally, west. "That's happened. Sometimes I like them, sometimes I don't. But that journey changed my life."

And, as Ronda explains to all kinds of audiences, it's all about the journey.

Six

Legacy and Souvenirs

This is where it all ends.

There's a small sign, down on the path, that reads, "Welcome to the Edge of the Continent," but visitors hardly need it. Not only is there an interpretive center a few yards away, but the place itself—where southwest Washington juts into the Pacific, leading with its chin—carries its identity as if the cliffs were made of neon.

This is the point, 200 feet up from the surf, where—after a year and a half, 5,000 miles, countless and unexpected mountains, and endless stomach-churning meals—Lewis and Clark and the Corps of Discovery met the Pacific. They had believed they had caught sight of the ocean days before, from just up the Columbia River, and now they went up the hill to face it directly in small groups.

In John Keats' imagining, in "On First Looking into Chapman's Homer," the Spanish who first saw the Pacific from Panama silently "Look'd at each other with a wild surmise." But in their first encounter with the Pacific, Lewis and Clark knew what it was and what it had cost them. The men, wrote Clark in November 1805, "appear much Satisfied with their trip, beholding with estonishment the high waves dashing across the rocks & this emence Ocian."

Exploring the coast, Lewis and Clark, like schoolboys loose after an endless term, carved their names on trees and gave names to hills and promontories.

The place, named Cape Disappointment in 1788 by Lieutenant John Meares of the British Royal Navy—who knew the Columbia River was there somewhere but couldn't quite find it—is now part of the newest element in the National Park Service system, the Lewis and Clark National Historical Park. Set up as part of the bicentennial, it adds Cape Disappointment and two other Lewis and Clark sites in Washington to Oregon's Fort Clatsop, where the Corps spent a winter Lewis wouldn't have wished on a Federalist.

The place where the trail runs into the Pacific has a particular magic to it. The National Park Service envisions Cape Disappointment as a match to Monticello and St. Louis' Gateway Arch, completing a triple tribute to Thomas Jefferson on the shore of an ocean he dreamed about and maneuvered toward—while himself never making it beyond the mountain range just past his Virginia porch.

The goal, explains Chip Jenkins, superintendent of the new park, was something that "uses the location, on the edge of a continent, to finish the thought. I don't think we're thinking monumental, a giant statue of Thomas Jefferson pointing west. We're thinking of a design by some really creative people of how this site encapsulates everything that way."

On the last two words, he jerks his thumb back behind him, back toward Monticello and St. Louis and all the rest of the trail, back toward all the time and space between this moment on the Pacific and Thomas Jefferson first imagining a nation that spanned a continent.

Nobody claims that someone standing here today sees what Lewis and Clark saw. Just past the newly overhauled interpretive center, there are thin strips of land setting off the mouth of the river, built up behind carefully assembled rock jetties that weren't there in 1805. Beyond them, frequently, are massive Japanese tankers, unimaginable extensions of the clipper ships on which Lewis and Clark vainly hoped to catch a ride home in 1806.

Just in front of the bluff a hawk rides the air currents, and an ocean of possibility stretches over the horizon. That part is still the same.

The Lewis and Clark National Historical Park straddles two states as well as a long-running Northwest argument about just where the trail ends—on the Washington side at Cape Disappointment or on the Oregon side at Fort Clatsop. The park also signifies a changing future for the mouth of the Columbia and for other places along the trail.

In Washington state, the expanded national park also adds Clark's Dismal Nitch, where the Corps found itself isolated and assaulted by a raging Columbia, and Station Camp, where its members voted to head across the river to find a place to spend the winter. (In early 2005, archaeological digging on the site found evidence of Chinook trading with Europeans before the Corps of Discovery arrived, slowing down the project's road relocation.) Since the decision to cross the river for the winter set off the historical disagreement over where the trail ended—a disagreement between two states that in 1805 weren't even a gleam in Jefferson's eye—an administrative reconnection of the two sides finally settles the argument.

Where does the trail end? At the Lewis and Clark National Historical Park.

The re-imagined Cape Disappointment includes the opening statement of Maya Lin's Confluence Project, designed for formal opening on the 200th anniversary of Clark's finally facing his objective.

Across the river at Fort Clatsop, in Oregon, the expanded park includes a tenfold expansion of the Park Service territory and a new trail from the re-created fort to where Lewis and Clark drew salt from the ocean. It's a trail that travels through time as well as distance. Walking to a place where men in buckskins boiled ocean water for salt, visitors will pass under Oregon's main coastal highway and along the rim of the Astoria Golf and Country Club.

It took a major local effort, a few years before, to keep the salt site itself from becoming a golf course—presenting Lewis and Clark with one last set of water hazards.

To Chip Jenkins, the expansion is a way to get visitors out of the fort and the gift shop, "to get out into the area, to get a sense of what 200 years has meant to the area, the expedition and the tribes." To get the most sweeping view, he suggests, tourists could go up to the Astoria Column overlooking the city and the mouth of the Columbia and see everything from the remains of an Ice Age flood to the ocean shipping of 21st-century Toyotas.

They could also see a transforming economy. Astoria is becoming a vivid illustration of how a western "extractive economy" now refers less to the land than to travelers' wallets. Besides a rise in Lewis and Clark tourism, Astoria now hosts hundreds of cruise ships a year and is becoming an attraction to people who can live anywhere with a high-speed computer connection and a nearby airport. All of it hangs on a future of maintaining environment and livability, not harvesting it.

It's a future to think about, thinks Jenkins, particularly while looking off the edge of Cape Disappointment.

"The Oregon Territory encapsulated the West," he says, looking out to sea as if searching for a ship, or an answer. "You can come here and think about the next 200 years, and wonder what's the Oregon territory of the future. Space? Stars? Between our ears?"

The place, he figures, tells visitors one thing: "We don't have any farther west to go."

The profile, gazing off at something not to be seen, is a nickel-familiar Indian portrait, all dignity and endurance and beads. The model is a Pacific Northwest tribal elder. But the picture looks like it could be from anywhere on the continent, and the pamphlet looks like something already well-known across America.

Inside, it's a little less predictable.

"We have a lot to show you. Welcome to our homelands," declares the opening. "In the face of enormous challenge and hardship we have survived. We are remarkable nations and we have remarkable stories to tell."

As a come-on, it's not exactly "I Love New York" or "What Happens in Vegas, Stays in Vegas." But even without the background music and dancing graphics, the pamphlet sets out a potentially historic landmark: the tribal tourism trail.

The pamphlet has a mouth-filling title—*A Guide to Visiting the Lands of Many Nations & to the Lewis & Clark Bicentennial.* Covering Indian Country all along the trail, it offers a lot of useful travel tips on attractions and amenities, on which reservations have casinos and which have gift shops, but it is considerably more than a tribal Triple-A guide.

Along with hundreds of useful phone numbers (to reach the Yakama Nations Legends Casino in Toppenish, Washington, call 877-7COME11), it's an etiquette guide to visiting Indian lands, a listing of the different bands in each tribe, and a calendar of celebrations, rodeos, and powwows.

But the handbook, published by the Circle of Tribal Advisors, also offers something you won't get in a guide to Disneyland or Colonial Williamsburg—a polite but unflinching statement of how your hosts see the world.

"There are thousands of tribal cultural resource areas, burial grounds and sacred sites along the Lewis & Clark National Historic Trail," the handbook explains, sounding like a glossy come-hither resort brochure—before making a sharp turn toward principle.

"The destruction, desecration, excavation, looting, vandalism and theft of these cultural resource areas, archaeological sites, burial grounds and sacred sites are a national disgrace.... Our sacred sources are monuments. And like the monuments of all great nations, they deserve respect."

Oregon Governor Tom McCall became famous forever for telling the world in 1971: "Come visit us again and again. But for heaven's sake, don't come here to live." The tribes of the Lewis and Clark Trail send an even more heartfelt message: Please visit, but for heaven's sake don't dig.

A Guide to Visiting the Lands of Many Nations & to the Lewis & Clark Bicentennial makes that kind of statement and has drawn the kind of response that defines it as a landmark legacy of the bicentennial. At the end of 2004, the first printing of 100,000 was gone, and COTA was scrabbling for grants for a second printing of 250,000. The brochure could also be downloaded from the bicentennial Web site.

"People are picking it up at every single event," said Sammye Meadows, cultural awareness coordinator at the Bicentennial Council. "It's going faster than any other brochure."

The people who pick it up gather a great deal of information. In addition to casinos, reservations have colleges and art galleries, and virtually all tribes have regular powwows—competitive dance events with food, clothing, and arts booths traveling around on a powwow circuit. Some powwows are specifically in honor of a tribe's military veterans; just about all will make a point of honoring a tribe's members who have served—often in sizable proportions—from Guadalcanal to Baghdad. When a Navajo woman died in the early days of the Iraq war, representatives of other tribes journeyed to Arizona to pay their respects.

The pamphlet lists annual historical commemorations held by many tribes, including a Custer's Last Stand pageant by the Crow in Montana. The Cheyenne River Sioux offer buffalo, wild-horse, and elk tours on their local reserve. The Absentee Shawnee Tribe in Oklahoma—they're not on the trail now, but they were in 1803—has a tribal golf course.

The information comes with the tribes' traditional Indian names, phone numbers, and Web sites.

And an invitation.

"Are you welcome to visit tribal communities and locations? *Absolutely!* We have been welcoming visitors—Indian and non-Indian—to our communities since the beginning of time. When visiting, please treat our home as you would anyone else's—with a respect for property, privacy and traditions."

Some ceremonies will be private, the pamphlet advises. Ask permission before taking pictures; don't just wander into private homes—which, somehow, tribal officials insist, visitors sometimes feel free to do on reservations.

"It's common sense, really. So enjoy your visit, and come back again and again."

Because no tourist experience is complete without a souvenir, there is a guide to buying Indian art, an increasingly fashionable genre, from southwestern pots to Arctic whale-tooth carvings. "Our arts are distinct, and our artists are respected and valued," explains the brochure, and then offers some tips, advising shoppers to ask for documentation, know what they're buying, and understand that, whatever the movies suggest, not every Indian artist is willing to haggle.

The careful combination of pride and instruction marks another small step in a deliberate tribal mainstreaming, an attempt to present Indians not as anthropological exotics but as different societies to be visited, valued, and placed into travelers' experience.

Presenting them, in fact, as nations.

Which is why—unlike, say, the Frommer guide to Italy—this one guide also has a section entitled, "A Treaty Is a Formal Contract Between Sovereign Nations." And why, every so often, it will pause to remind tourists, "Be aware that every landscape you experience continues to be a tribal homeland."

The connection between the tribes of western legend and the tribes of western present isn't always understood.

"People saw *Dances with Wolves,* or they see us as the people who tried to shoot John Wayne; they don't see us as modern people," says Meadows. "The descendants of the people who met Lewis and Clark are still there, and they're doctors and lawyers and ballerinas. They wear Nikes and they play basketball in school. They're not scary people, and they're not ghosts."

Of course, there is that long history about the cavalry and the diseases and the removals, and that does come up.

"I'd like to see a real national dialogue on what this country was built on," says Meadows. "It was built on genocide."

So, *A Guide to Visiting the Lands of Many Nations & to the Lewis & Clark Bicentennial* is a significant effort to reach out to a different tribal future, but it still has to help grapple with everything from the past.

Meadows pauses after she explains it. "That's a lot to expect," she admits, "from one brochure."

Then again, it's not a bashful brochure.

"We are proud peoples," it declares. "We are proud of our traditions, languages, arts and histories. We are proud of our achievements and contributions to American society, including those to the Lewis & Clark Expedition. We are part of this great American landscape. We come from these lands, and we will always be here."

It is, in its basic identity, just a book, borrowed from a friend and returned three years later, probably to someone who quietly told himself he'd be more careful about the people he lent it to in the future. But in the national Lewis and Clark exhibit crisscrossing the country for three years from 2004 to 2006, *The History of Louisiana* was the first object people encountered that actually went on the Corps' journey across the continent.

Exhibit-goers looked at the book and thought about it going up the Missouri, across the Rockies, to the Pacific, and then back. Inside is an inscription from Meriwether Lewis to the owner of the book, just as someone might express appreciation for a book loaned for a week at the lake—except that this note explains that after Lewis borrowed the volume, "it has been since conveyed by me to the Pacific Ocean through the interior of the continent of North America on my journey thither."

As the Indians often told the explorers, objects can have magic. The drawing power of 200-year-old souvenirs—the Missouri Historical Society, the show's assembler and first exhibitor, had to cut down the number of timed tickets it sold, because visitors spent more time in the exhibit than anyone had expected—was part of the impact of the Lewis and Clark bicentennial and part of its enduring message.

By the time the exhibit completes its two-and-a-half-year trip back and forth across the country—St. Louis to Philadelphia to Denver to Portland to Washington, D.C., a zigzag path that makes the expedition's trip look like a straight shot down an interstate—as many as a million people will have seen the book and more than 500 other artifacts. The collection has the power not only to make visitors careful about lending out their books, but also to make them think about people who could paddle and climb their way almost the length of a continent.

They will also think about what happens when one culture encounters another—especially when one of the cultures is vastly more advanced in weaponry.

It's an issue that, somewhere out past the moon, could come up again at any moment.

Lewis & Clark: The National Bicentennial Exhibition set out two themes, themes that gave any of its million visitors something to think about even after leaving the gift shop. Five hundred different pieces on display allow space for both history and heroism.

The technological gap was drawn in iron. There are samples of the expedition's long rifle, the blunderbuss, the swivel gun from the boat, pistols, and Lewis' air gun, also exhibited at Monticello. Tribes would have recognized the theory of the U.S. Army espontoon, a semi-ceremonial spear, but not its precision ironwork. The weaponry is only a relatively small piece of the exhibition, but it caught the strolling viewer. It made everything else possible.

Other devices can declare mastery without bloodshed. The direct line forward to a different West—and backward to Jefferson—was marked by the exhibition's scientific instruments. Visitors scanned Lewis' telescope, a compass, a surveyor's device, a chronometer that may or may not have been his. The instruments represent the capacity—and the Enlightenment imperative—to measure, order, and classify reality, to begin to bend it to the measurers' will.

None of the dozens and dozens of dazzling evocations of tribal life carry that particular message. The Indian artifacts include elaborately worked buffalo robes, bone tools for hides, beaded clothing, and heart-stirring war shirts. They are the direct ancestors of the tribal artwork promoted in the COTA travel guide.

Tattered from two centuries, the artifacts survived to declare vividly that Lewis and Clark were not exploring a wilderness. They showed that the tribal West encountered by the expedition included cultures of elaborate and subtle artwork and social organization, and that without them the Corps of Discovery would never have seen the Pacific.

But the tribes' view of the world, a view of richness and existence drawn from close connection with nature, was not the outlook of the men of the Lewis and Clark expedition. The exhibit lays out a contrast of cultures that, among other implications, rendered the eventual clash of cultures so technologically uneven.

The evidence of this situation most apparent to field-tripping fifth graders, of course, sets the keelboat swivel gun against the tribal battle axe. But the exhibit's most striking examples, set against each other, were the two cultures' maps, their explanations of the world around them.

The tribal maps exhibited are almost anecdotal, compressing space, listing natural landmarks, and sometimes identifying the wildlife likely to be encountered along the way. The maps drawn by Clark, even freehand in the midst of a North Dakota winter, are careful and measured, with distance calculated on gridded paper and river bends portrayed as from a helicopter.

Both kinds of maps fit the purposes of their producers—and, in a metaphor for the entire experience, the expedition's maps often relied on the tribal maps. But one kind of map is about fitting into the landscape, the other about ordering and mastering it.

Clark's maps, you might say, are as precise as a rifle shot.

The exhibit provides other pieces of paper about power, including the most chilling one: an advertisement, dated February 22, 1809, St. Louis, reading, "I wish to SELL two likely NEGRO MEN for Cash. William Clark."

The advertisement was printed two and a half years after the expedition returned, but it said something loudly about the status of one member of the Corps.

At the beginning of the bicentennial, Lewis and Clark enthusiasts found a major new theme in York, Clark's slave, who accompanied him on the trip and played an important role as both a strong and resourceful expedition member and a source of fascination to the Indians. The years approaching the bicentennial saw books (adult's and children's) on York, at least one documentary, and a dramatic statue of him on the riverfront in Louisville—although there are no images to suggest what York looked like.

Some even hoped that York's physical anonymity might contribute to his universality as a symbol.

Ron Craig of Portland, author of *Who Was York?*, told the Monticello crowd about visiting a Washington, D.C., school and being asked by a young boy what York looked like and why there weren't any pictures of him. Craig walked the boy over to a mirror and told him that what he saw was what York looked like.

There was a widely expressed anticipation, or at least a hope, that York—more prominent in the 2005 version of story than the ones told over the previous two centuries—could stir African-American interest in the bicentennial. But from early on, there was little evidence of that happening.

The answer, possibly, was not about York's role in the expedition but about the advertisement offering two of Clark's slaves for sale. However impressive the accounts of what York did on the expedition, they are still overshadowed by what he was.

York's efforts were prodigious, but he was the only member of the expedition not to receive land or any other reward on its completion. Even on the trail, York was a man owned by another man, a man who had the power to beat or sell him—two options that did not come up on the expedition but apparently did after Clark and York returned to St. Louis. Clark spent a decade complaining about York's attitude, sometimes beating him and indifferent or hostile to York's own wishes. Wrote Brian Hall, author of the popular bicentennial novel of the expedition, *I Should Be Very Happy in Your Company*, in a special *Time* bicentennial issue: "Clark's callousness toward York sits awkwardly with his portrayal as an American hero."

After a prominent role in the expedition, York returned to the United States only to the possibility of being one more likely Negro man available to be sold for cash. That fact may not make him less heroic, but it may make him a more difficult figure to identify with—or lead to a more painful identification.

"York crossed the river, he crossed the mountains, he saw what freedom meant," James Ronda told a television audience. "And then re-entered a world of slavery where slavery was everywhere."

York as a member of the expedition—although a member without image or artifact or reward—clearly deserves the expanded attention he now gets. But as a symbol of diversity, and of an African-American involvement in the Lewis and Clark saga, the story of York may be unable to bear the burden the 21st century wants to put on it.

Even if he did get a vote on whether the Corps would spend the winter on the Pacific.

History can be empowering. But it can also be inescapable.

The Lewis and Clark exhibition's 500 artifacts of the expedition were seen, or at least encountered, by hundreds of thousands of visitors—creating millions and millions of possible connections, potential shards of history sticking under someone's skin. It's a legacy that won't show up on a 2006 balance sheet. But it is a considerable legacy, and part of a story that reminds us that outcomes and implications can outrun not only calculation but also imagination.

One of the most immediately, and bureaucratically, recognizable documents of the exhibit is Lewis' handwritten proposed budget, declaring that the expedition could be brought off for $2,500. Scrupulously, he breaks down the details: $217 for mathematical instruments, $696 for presents for the tribes en route.

Like similar government estimates before and since, Lewis' was a little low. The expedition ended up costing the government about $38,000.

Two hundred years later, Representative David Wu, the congressman representing Fort Clatsop, sat in his office on Capitol Hill and cited the Lewis and Clark budget as an example of how government spending may go higher than expected but can produce benefits beyond anything imagined.

Lewis and Clark's route to the Pacific Ocean never produced, as they had hoped, a water route to the Pacific and then on to the rich trade of China. But 200 years later, their trail ends in a West beyond their imagining, a West of inconceivable diversity and international influence, in a nation outside the furthest expectations of the two Jeffersonian Virginians who first crossed it.

The Northwest is still not reachable by a water route that leads on to Asia. But the bicentennial exhibit arrived there to find something much more distant from 1805 Washington than China itself—a Chinese-American congressman.

What's outside a museum can be more striking than anything displayed inside.

Nobody ever just happened to come by south-central North Dakota. The land is flat, the landscape runs to corn and pasture, the interstate rolls on forever, and the horizon in the distance might be Saskatchewan. The winters run to snow, the summers run to mosquitoes, and in the population rankings of the 50 states, North Dakota is 47th and dropping.

People need to make an effort to come here, and usually—like Lewis and Clark—it's because they're on the way to someplace else.

But here, in the town of Washburn—38 miles north of Bismarck, with one motel and dining-out directions that include filling your gas tank first—there are large tour buses in the parking lot and license plates from places with major-league teams, kindly climates, and names that feature prominently in adolescents' dreams.

And the tour buses have come here to North Dakota, where no teenager has ever demanded to be taken.

"For generations, our strategy has been to slow people down on their way somewhere else," said David Borlaug in the summer of 2003, a few yards from the parking lot. "For the first time ever, we are a destination. Lewis and Clark is driving that. Eighty percent of our visitors say it's their first visit. That's why it's a sea change for North Dakota. This is forever."

North Dakota, of all the places hoping for a bicentennial bonanza of tourism—and a long-term repositioning—may be both the most remote and the most successful. Well into the commemoration, the state had seized the moment to turn heritage into heritage tourism.

Borlaug, head of the state's bicentennial effort and former three-year president of the national Bicentennial Council, is president of the

Lewis & Clark Fort Mandan Foundation, which operates the Lewis & Clark Interpretive Center in Washburn. It's on a hill just off I-83 and just up from the Missouri River—the road and the river are the two main drags of North Dakota—and it's just a few miles from a re-created Fort Mandan, the Corps' 1804-1805 winter quarters.

In 2003, the two attractions drew 22,000 visitors. In 2004, that more than doubled to 48,000—despite what everybody in North Dakota will tell you quickly was a damp, miserable summer.

Most of them, said Borlaug—striding quickly among the center's collections of tribal artifacts, 19th-century European paintings of the West, and interactive exhibits—have never been here before. He expects many of them to return and to send and bring their friends.

"In our business, the word spreads. I think we'll see wave after wave of growth in heritage tourism, and we'll look back and say it was the Lewis and Clark bicentennial," he said confidently. "Now we've got America's attention."

However long that attention lasts, North Dakota—once described by native son Eric Sevareid, the CBS News legend, as a "meaningless rectangle" on the top of the country—worked hard for it. Looking toward the bicentennial, North Dakotans opened the interpretive center in 1997. Borlaug joined in 2000, after working in his family's local newspaper business and a chain of agricultural papers, and the center operates with a publisher's nose for promotion. A statue of Sacagawea—or Sakakawea to the Mandan-Hidatsa—representing North Dakota, was donated to the U.S. Capitol in 2003, the center has added a statue of Lewis' dog Seaman, and in February 2005 it held a 200th birthday party for Sacagawea's son Jean Baptiste Charbonneau, or Pompey.

The reconstructed Fort Mandan itself claims, very plausibly, to have the most extensive and complete Lewis and Clark gift shop on the entire trail—viewed by Borlaug as part of the operation's educational mission.

As the bicentennial approached, the North Dakota legislature even joined the party, in an uncharacteristic way. It authorized a one percent lodging tax to pay for tourism promotion, featuring both the bicentennial and the state's Legends promotion—featuring Lewis and Clark, Sacagawea, Sitting Bull, George Armstrong Custer, and Theodore Roosevelt.

In Borlaug's view, "When they saw the way we took off, the state decided to ante up some more." At the far western edge of the state, North Dakota also opened, in 2003, the Missouri-Yellowstone Confluence Interpretive Center, which features Lewis and Clark's reconnection with each other on the way home.

North Dakota put on the largest promotion of any state at the bicentennial kickoff at Monticello. That event, and state tourism programs in general, have included major efforts by the Mandan-Hidatsa-Arikara Nation, whose stories are particularly compelling to visitors—particularly Europeans cherishing a Wild West that seems only more alluring for being an ocean away.

And tourism numbers are up, said Sara Coleman, director of the state Department of Commerce Tourism Division, in 2005—despite, of course, the disappointing summer weather. It's hard to say how much is entirely due to Lewis and Clark, but the Circle of Cultures Signature Event in Bismarck in November 2004 drew an unexpected 50,000 people—which, noted Borlaug, is a lot of people for North Dakota. (It would be the state's third largest city.)

And visitors weren't just looking thoughtfully at artifacts and re-creations. The Lewis and Clark riverboat ride on the Missouri—and ,okay, Lewis and Clark never rode a riverboat—was up 90 percent in 2004, and Birdwoman Canoe Adventures was up 40 percent over the previous year.

"It's helped us focus on what's important, the stories we have to tell," said Coleman. "Heritage is a huge part of our industry, and those travelers spend more and stay longer."

Coleman estimated that for every dollar the state spent on Lewis and Clark tourism promotion North Dakota got $83 back.

Nobody expects that North Dakota—or Montana or the Lower Brule Sioux Reservation or Pacific County, Washington—is about to become Las Vegas or a hot spring-break destination. But North Dakota, a poster state for Great Plains depopulation—the only state with fewer people than it had in 1930 and the only state with a population drop from 2000 to 2003—is a place in search of redefinition.

North Dakota is the most extreme example of many places along the trail, and around the West, looking for a different identity. An event that broadens the image of the state, that presents it as some-

thing beyond a "meaningless rectangle" of Norwegian wheat grow-
ers—70,000 square miles of Lake Wobegone—can suggest a different
image and future.

The bicentennial, said Borlaug, has brought in "tens of thousands
of people who 10 years ago never gave North Dakota a thought."

It even, he declared, made North Dakotans think. The bicentennial
was "a chance for our own people to get an appreciation of our depth of
cultural heritage, that we're not just Germans and Norwegians. Lewis
and Clark is just the beginning. We can continue telling stories."

Coming down the Columbia River, riding a fast current and facing
sudden Disneyland-level rapids, Lewis and Clark could barely take
their eyes off the river. Still, they could hardly avoid noticing the
overshadowing Mount Hood, described by Clark in October 1805 as "a
mountain bearing S.W. conical form Covered with Snow."

Two centuries later, the captains and the mountain would be
joined in the Lewis and Clark Mount Hood Wilderness Act, the first
and most striking potential environmental legacy of the bicentennial.
Rising in the Senate in March 2004, Senator Ron Wyden (D-Ore.) noted "the bicentennial of the single most important exploratory committee ever launched by the Federal Government and that is the Lewis
and Clark Expedition." He proposed his bill as "one way to mark this
very special time."

Wyden added: "In tribute to the great river-dependent journey
of Lewis and Clark, I believe it would also be appropriate to add four
free-flowing stretches of rivers to the National Wild and Scenic River
System."

With the fiscal and political conditions of the federal government,
the early activist goals of marking the bicentennial with considerable
expansions of federal wilderness along the trail became as unlikely as
a buffalo stampede through Omaha. But, appropriately for dealing
with lands and rivers, environmental goals are long-term goals, and
they build over years and over Congresses and administrations.

Besides, on lands that extend down the slopes of Mount Hood
toward the expedition's more recognizably riverside territory, there
are issues that never came up in 1805—such as mountain bikes and
making the wilderness handicapped-accessible. Skeptics about ex-

panding wilderness coverage in an area so close to an urban area, and so extensively used, asked—in the phrase of Oregon's other senator, Gordon Smith (R. Ore.)—whether the goal was to protect the land *for* people or *from* people.

Slowly, over a period that seemed likely to last longer than the expedition itself, Wyden worked to line up the rest of the state delegation, to reach out to the rest of Congress, to talk with the administration. Oregon House members held town-hall meetings to talk about the issue, and the Sierra Club and other groups worked to build support—including a billboard in Hood River, home of GOP Representative Greg Walden and right along the Lewis and Clark Trail, urging him to support the proposal.

To Wyden, Lewis and Clark provided a key momentum—both in Oregon, where they caught a local commitment to wild places, and in Washington, D.C. "Look at the number of people who belong to the Lewis and Clark Caucus," Wyden said a year after introducing his bill. "I'm amazed how much someone like Senator Dorgan [Democrat Byron L. Dorgan of North Dakota] knows about Lewis and Clark."

A lot of environmental themes have support. Not many have their own caucus.

Dorgan's North Dakota has its own bicentennial environmental priorities, and its own bicentennial environmental activists. The Garrison Reach on the Missouri, between the Garrison Dam and Lake Owyhee, runs for 80 miles, the longest free-flowing stretch of the river between St. Louis and the Montana state line. Protecting it—and its piping plovers, its interior least terns, and its historic sites—tops the local Lewis and Clark list.

"Since we started this campaign," said Jonathan Bry of the state Sierra Club about its bicentennial effort, "there's been a lot more awareness of the importance of the river to the expedition, more interest in going canoeing on the river, seeing what it looked like to the Corps of Discovery. Lewis and Clark buffs really do want to protect the river."

Bry grew up in North Dakota along the Missouri, went to San Francisco for college, and eventually came back—for largely riparian reasons. "If it wasn't for the river," he said with soft certainty, "I wouldn't be living here."

The bicentennial effort helped stir a new group, the Friends of the Missouri River—"a separate operation, but I would have to say it was very much influenced by the bicentennial," explained Bry. The Sierra Club itself now has a Missouri River working group, with members from each of the seven states along the river. "We're not exactly sure how we're going to go about this," admitted Bry. "We would eventually like to see some federal legislation that would protect the Missouri River. That's a ways away."

Of course, the thing about a 200-year commemoration is it gives you some perspective. And in the West, not every route goes through Washington, D.C.

Like some other state legislatures, the 2005 session of the Montana legislature—a legislature newly controlled by Democrats, probably as much to their surprise as anyone else's—passed its own Lewis and Clark resolution. It applauded the expedition and Jefferson, hailed the tribal contribution to the journey, and "supported Montana's efforts to encourage all Americans to visit."

But it also made some other points, declaring that "in the span of 200 years since the Lewis and Clark expedition, the Missouri River has been dammed and transformed into a series of slack-water impoundments, or in many places, narrow, fast-flowing channels, and management of this river significantly affects the continuance of agriculture, fisheries, wildlife and recreation." The legislature resolved to "support the Missouri River through science-based management of its annual water fluctuations and maintenance of its fisheries and wildlife populations" and to "support the conservation of our natural heritage as a commemoration of the spirit of the Corps of Discovery."

Montana is a divided state, says the resolution's sponsor, state Representative Bob Bergren of Havre—up on the north side of the state on what Montanans call the Hi-Line. In fact, the House elected in 2004 split 50-50, a tie that gave the new Democratic governor the power to name the Speaker.

The division of the state, Bergren noted, makes additional federal wilderness a tough sell, but he would be open to the idea. "I go up into the Bob Marshall Wilderness, one of the most beautiful places on earth," he said, "and I think that's precious."

In the state House, Bergren—a firefighter, small businessman, and House whip—maneuvered his resolution through by a vote of 98-2.

Republicans, Bergren recalls, "were raising their eyebrows" at the beginning, and the resolution may not have as many teeth or specifics as it might have. But he kept everyone on board, including a number of Indian legislators who had nothing against the environment but had some doubts about Lewis and Clark, and Bergren thinks the resolution sends a message.

"The most important thing is the science-based preservation of the rivers and streams," said Bergren. "Hopefully, when we see legislation, they'll recognize that, and we won't be damaging those things."

On water or land, there is a particular Lewis and Clark power in Montana, where the state capital is in Lewis and Clark County.

"They say that in Montana we have some of the largest parts of the trail that are closest to what they saw," said Bergren. "We'd like to preserve that for future generations."

In the summer of 2002, when the organizational structure of the bicentennial crumbled, there was a major wild card in the Missouri Historical Society's consideration of whether to make a huge bet of its own money to stabilize the operation.

The central questions of 1805 America—what was out there in the West, and what it could it mean?—merged into the central question of 2005 America: Can you get on television?

It seemed the Lewis and Clark bicentennial could. And even bring someone else along.

By the time Robert Archibald led the Missouri Historical Society in taking over the bicentennial, the Bicentennial Council had acquired at least one major asset. The Lewis and Clark bicentennial had been accepted as a public-service ad campaign by the Ad Council, Madison Avenue's pro bono wing. The arrangement dangled the possibility of more than $100 million in free TV, radio, and print advertising.

When a cause is accepted, the Ad Council finds an interested ad agency. The cause itself pays the up front expenses of production, and the Ad Council places the ads with media outlets that run them at no charge as public-service announcements. Three years of those placements could expose more Americans to the Lewis and Clark bicentennial than all of the carefully planned Signature Events put together.

Americans, after all, watch a lot of television. They also listen to a lot of radio and even still read some newspapers.

So, beginning in 2004, Americans all over the country—people far from the trail and people with no idea where the trail might be—could look at their TV screens and be told how the Lewis and Clark story showed the values of leadership, teamwork, and mentoring or how the tribes that met the expedition are still around. They might hear on their radios, between spots for auto-body companies and diet supplements, 30-second spots about Sacagawea or York. Turning a magazine or newspaper page revealed print ads headed, "The Farther they Got from Civilization, the More Civilized they Became or "Imagine a Military Expedition Notable for the Battles that Didn't Happen."

Lewis and Clark, who in life produced one book that yielded Clark a total of $180 in royalties, had become mass-media celebrities.

Through the third quarter of 2004—the early edge of the bicentennial—the Ad Council campaign drew more than $30 million in donated media time and space, mostly on radio. By the second year, evolving as fast as the media scene itself, the campaign was running bicentennial ads and links on newspaper Web sites and a two-page spread in *Sports Illustrated*. Among more than 40 Ad Council campaigns running at the same time, the Council counted the Lewis and Clark effort in its highest tier of visibility. The ads were intended to draw people to the bicentennial Web site, lewisandclark200.org, which through 2004 averaged between 35,000 and 50,000 visits a month.

Maybe not Drudge Report numbers, but nobody was complaining.

"We're very pleased with the coverage we've seen," said Karen Goering of the Missouri Historical Society, executive director of the Bicentennial Council. "We're seeing a pickup in people coming to the site. Some of the biggest markets have been nowhere near the trail," notably in the Southwest and on the East Coast.

Which was where what may be the Lewis and Clark bicentennial's biggest thumbprint on the American consciousness was devised—in a city neither of the captains ever visited, a place where the territory they covered by foot and boat is generally referred to as flyover country.

"We didn't want it to be a history lesson," explained James Othmar, a senior vice president and creative director at Young & Rubicam in New York, who oversaw the development of the campaign. "As for what we could learn from it, what are the socially redeeming points, that was a challenge."

The idea of a Lewis and Clark impact on the present was inherent in the slogan that concluded each ad: "Walk with them and see what you discover." The campaign, said Othmar, was about "the idea that from this, you can become a better person, and make this a better country."

It was only the part after that that got complicated.

In his time at Young & Rubicam, Othmar had worked on ad campaigns for AT&T, Accenture, Intel, and General Motors. Besides more money, those efforts had another advantage on the bicentennial—a single constituency.

This time it was more complicated, even after Othmar went to the opening event at Monticello to get an idea of the themes involved.

There were tribal constituencies, environmental constituencies, historians, state tourism agencies, and old-line Lewis and Clark buffs—and they all had to be satisfied by ads that lasted 30 seconds.

"To me it was kind of fascinating, the type of people I was dealing with," said Othmar. "We're on the other side of the country. Whatever we picked had some complication to it. People would push back."

And sometimes they would sniff that yuppies living in Manhattan couldn't understand the issues or the West.

The first effort at an environmental theme was rejected by both environmentalists and some western state officials, and the mood wasn't helped by a newspaper story about the dispute. Because of the difficulty in reaching consensus, ads with an environmental theme—focusing on animals that were threatened but still hanging in there—wouldn't appear until the second year of the bicentennial.

Indian themes were even more complex, with different tribal constituencies who each had their own issues. Othmar, with his wife and daughter, went out to a Crow reservation in Wyoming to shoot the spots, "one of the best experiences I ever had in advertising."

For each piece, there were implications and questions. The theme, "The Farther they Got from Civilization, the More Civilized they Became," made some Indians uncomfortable with the idea that going into tribal territory, Lewis and Clark were leaving civilization. The warmly received, and widely run, spot, "200 years ago, Lewis and Clark discovered the West—that is if you don't count the 2 million people who discovered it first," raised objections from some COTA members that their tribes never discovered their homeland—they had always been there.

And watching the 30-second "Discovery" TV spot, which focused on modern Indians, some committee members expressed concern that nobody was smiling—which did not exactly make for an inviting tourist appeal.

Commented Othmar, "I thought that was an interesting nuance." Eventually, "I think they came around, and they saw we got it."

There were concerns in Manhattan, as well. When Othmar taped the Sacagawea radio spot—featuring the Inupiat/Cree actress Irene Bedard, who did the voice-over for Disney's *Pocahontas*—people around him "kept saying, 'Can she sound more Indian?' I wasn't going to ask her to do that."

Agency concerns eased when one of the ads was short-listed for a public-service award at the Cannes Film Festival. "Then, suddenly, everyone in the agency was asking about it, trying to claim credit."

There was one direct way to have the spots sound more Indian— have them made by Indians. And COTA also went that route.

With some grant money, COTA commissioned a second set of bicentennial public-service ads, working with a group at the University of Montana and G+G Advertising of Albuquerque, New Mexico, and Billings, Montana. The spots by G+G, which calls itself the only Indian-owned full-service ad agency in the country, are part of the bicentennial's official offerings and available on its Web site.

G+G focuses more directly on tribal themes: survival, respect for Indian property, land stewardship. The ads show only Indians and present only tribal voices.

In the "Survival" spot, a half-dozen voices, from elders to children, talk about the tribes' endurance and determination to survive, including the message, "Our survival is your survival." The spot entitled "Respect," focusing on artifacts being taken from tribal lands—an issue that repeatedly comes up almost immediately with tribes—begins by filling up the screen with American iconic places, from battlefields to the Lincoln Memorial, and warning that if every visitor took something from each place, there would soon be nothing left of any of them.

"Non-Indian advertising companies really don't know anything about Indian country," said Gerald Gray, Sr., a partner in G+G. "We wanted to make sure the messages were coming from the Native Americans themselves. The topics were serious, but we wanted to make sure the ads didn't scare people off. I think a long-term legacy of this campaign is that Indians are reaching out for the first time, and asking people to come and visit."

The Ad Council and the COTA campaign together create a new kind of bicentennial legacy, something not seen in previous commemorations, something different even from the 1976 TV "Bicentennial Minutes." For three years, people would listen to the radio or watch television or look at a magazine and be urged to think about how a historical event shaped their lives—and how it should shape their future.

Americans manage to combine a deep reverence for their past with a minimal knowledge of it, gathered from fading high school memories, vague invocations offered by politicians, and period recreations they once saw on television. (Increasingly, it also comes from RV trips to historical points, another stream being fed by the bicentennial.) A campaign repeatedly invoking a major piece of the past and insisting on its relevance to the present, bringing up history in the style of advertising repetition rather than a swift bolt to a Friday quiz, could raise both memories and questions.

It is an approach that could raise, in James Othmar's modest formulation, "the idea that you can become a better person, and make this a better country."

Which history, after all, is supposed to do.

There are, on the bicentennial Web site and at every place where the trail tracks, a boatload of T-shirts, ball caps, and everything else that can be printed with the names "Lewis and Clark." From Indiana west to Idaho, the bicentennial will leave behind hundreds of thousands of Lewis and Clark license plates, all carrying a certain cargo of irony.

From the U.S. Capitol to Washington's Pacific Coast, the bicentennial is leaving behind enough statues for a pigeon plenary session.

These are all the most visible bicentennial bequests, the place where legacies intersect with souvenirs. There is nothing wrong with souvenirs, and a list of notable U.S. commemoration souvenirs includes the Seattle Space Needle (1962 World's Fair) and the Statue of Liberty (a gift for the centennial of the Declaration of Independence, although, like a lot of holiday presents, it was a little late getting set up). Often, a souvenir is as much legacy as you might expect from a commemoration—which is, after all, history twice removed.

A souvenir carries you back and a legacy carries you forward, and the themes of the Lewis and Clark bicentennial will roll across the West throughout the 21st century.

It is unquestionably the first major national occasion—let alone one lasting three years—with the active involvement of 60 tribal groups. The bicentennial carried national media advertising on the themes of tribal endurance and importance and dozens of new local interactions, from Signature Events to statewide tourism strategies, and created new ties and relationships between established power structures and tribal worlds. From Corps II to each bicentennial event, tribal voices declare that there is another side to the established narrative of the West—and even to the Lewis and Clark journals.

It is not a revolution, but it's an opening.

For the tribes, the bicentennial comes at the right time, not just the chronologically accurate moment. The bicentennial effort draws on a changing white attitude toward tribal history, which began in the 1960s, exemplified by the work of James Ronda. It also rides on a new wave of politically savvy, educated tribal members, reflected in a Circle of Tribal Advisors skilled at operating in both worlds.

Not to mention that, in virtually every trail state, casino revenues bring tribes closer to the political and economic table.

At the turn of the 21st century, at the coming of the bicentennial, the land itself was changing under the westerners' feet. After 200 years of operating as a natural resource economy, the West is seeing many of those industries fade, moving the region to turn more to lifestyle and recreation resources. It's a time for a repositioning, arriving fittingly at the bicentennial of explorers who were given—and who dazzlingly carried out—a mandate to depict the natural world they found in the West.

What started in the late 1990s as an ambitious environmental agenda was buffeted by major national and political events, including the elections of President George W. Bush, the draining attacks of 9/11, and the re-election defeat of Senate Democratic leader Tom Daschle of South Dakota.

The idea that politics can change a situation should hardly surprise commemorators of an expedition launched directly by Thomas Jefferson's election as president. But major underlying trends still outlast election returns. If John Adams had beaten Jefferson in 1800, the United States still wouldn't have stayed permanently east of the Mississippi.

On the environment as on the tribes, Lewis and Clark is a conversation starter among people who have spent a lot of energy not talking to each other.

The bicentennial has one more force to bring different Americans together—thousands of miles of trail, a hundred tourism strategies, and heritage tourists looking for something besides a motel.

Waves of minivans, Elderhostel buses, and recreational vehicles follow the trail like a Lewis and Clark cleanup crew. They stop at interpretive centers and restored forts. They watch—and buy from—blacksmiths and leather workers and people who sell linsey-woolsey britches.

Americans believe in journeys—not so much in arrivals, which are often followed by new departures, as in the journeys themselves. Heritage tourism connects not only the past and the present, but also different parts of the country, and the West's buffalo-and-logging past to a more recreational future.

Making the effort doubly connective is that heritage tourists are not only bringing something, notably money, but also looking for something, an identity and a past—both a visitable past and a bequeathable past. Vacations and pilgrimages have been blurring together at least since *The Canterbury Tales*, and 21st-century Americans are very big on multi-tasking.

The Lewis and Clark bicentennial arrived at a moment of dramatic change throughout the West and infused it with three years of mass media, events, and exhibitions injecting the past into the present. From St. Louis to the Pacific Coast, the bicentennial provided a moment when the question of how we got here shapes the answer of where we go next.

At least it avoided a national wave of souvenirs proclaiming, "My country marked the Lewis and Clark Bicentennial, and all I got was this crummy T-shirt."

Note on Photographs

Title page   Columbia River, looking downriver just below the mouth of the Snake, April 2004.

Pages 2-3   "Lewis and Clark on Their Way to the Pacific in 1805," 1938, mural by Barry Faulkner and Frank H. Schwarz, Oregon State Capitol, Legislative Administration. Courtesy of Oregon State Archives, Salem.

Page 10   Gerard Baker, Superintendent, Mount Rushmore National Memorial, National Park Service photo by Jeffrey G. Olson.

Pages 16-17   Commencement of the National Lewis & Clark Bicentennial Commemoration at Monticello, Virginia, January 18, 2003. Courtesy of Monticello/Thomas Jefferson Foundation.

Page 31   Dr. Robert R. Archibald, Ph.D., President and CEO of the Missouri Historical Society and President of the National Council of the Lewis & Clark Bicentennial. Courtesy of the Missouri Historical Society, St. Louis.

Pages 38-9   Commencement of the National Lewis & Clark Bicentennial Commemoration at Monticello, Virginia, January 18, 2003. Courtesy of Monticello/Thomas Jefferson Foundation.

Page 61   Roberta "Bobbie" Conner, Director, Tamástslikt Cultural Institute and Vice President of the National Council of the Lewis & Clark Bicentennial. Courtesy of Tamástslikt Cultural Institute.

Pages 68-9   "The Three Forks, Headwaters of the Missouri," by Alfred Edward Mathews, in *Pencil Sketches of Montana*, 1868. Courtesy of the Montana Historical Society, Helena.

Page 87   Mary Kiesau, former Project Manager, "Wild America: Protecting the Lands of Lewis and Clark," American Rivers. Courtesy of Mary Kiesau.

Pages 94-5   Keelboat Reenactment, St. Charles, Missouri, Jim Sturm, photographer. Courtesy of Jim Sturm.

Page 116   Maya Lin, sculptor, at one of the sites of the Confluence Project, Kent Derek, photographer. Courtesy of Kent Derek and the Confluence Project.

Pages 122-3   Living historians at "Salt Makers Return" program, National Park Service and Seaside Musuem, July 16, 2005, Seaside, Oregon. Left to right: Aaron Webster as Pvt. Rueben Fields, Tom Wilson as Pvt. William Bratten, and Roben Estes as Pvt. Alexander Willard.

Page 140   James P. Ronda, H.G. Barnard Professor of Western American History, The University of Tulsa, Jeanne Ronda, photographer. Courtesy of James P. Ronda.

Pages 146-7   Cape Disappointment, Washington State Parks and Recreation Commission.

Note on Sources

Most of the quotations, observations and visceral reactions in *Waiting for Lewis and Clark* came from my own reporting, from attendance at Bicentennial Council meetings, travel across the trail and the country, and frequent phone calls to people involved. Every one of them responded with a helpfulness and patience that can probably be expected only about once every 200 years.

I also drew a great deal of assistance from newspaper coverage of the bicentennial, notably *The Oregonian*, the *St. Louis Post-Dispatch*, the *Omaha World-Herald*, *The Washington Post*, *The New York Times*, the *Great Falls (Montana) Tribune*, the *Spokane Spokesman-Review* and the *Vancouver (Washington) Columbian*. If Lewis and Clark had had Nexis, their trip would have been a lot simpler.

I was hugely assisted by much of the core literature on the expedition and the West, notably the following:

John Logan Allen, *Passage through the Garden: Lewis and Clark and the Image of the American Northwest* (Springfield: University of Illinois Press, 1974).

Stephen E. Ambrose, *Undaunted Courage: Meriwether Lewis, Thomas Jefferson, and the Opening of the American West* (New York: Simon & Schuster, 1997).

Daniel B. Botkin, *Our Natural History: Lessons from Lewis and Clark* (New York: Putnam, 1995).

Bernard DeVoto, *The Course of Empire* (Boston: Houghton Mifflin Co., 1952).

Ian Frazier, *Great Plains* (New York: Farrar Straus Giroux, 1989).

Guy Gibbon, *The Sioux* (Malden: Blackwood, 2003).

Carolyn Gilman, *Lewis and Clark: Across the Divide* (Washington, D.C.: Smithsonian Books and Missouri Historical Society Press, 2003).

Donald Jackson, *Thomas Jefferson and the Stony Mountains: Exploring the West from Monticello* (Springfield: University of Illinois Press, 1981).

Landon Y. Jones, *William Clark and the Shaping of the West* (New York: Hill and Wang, 2004).

James Ronda, ed., *Finding the West: Explorations with Lewis and Clark* (Albuquerque: University of New Mexico Press, 2001).

James Ronda, *Lewis and Clark Among the Indians* (Lincoln: University of Nebraska Press, 1984).

Hal K. Rothman, *Devil's Bargains: Tourism in the Twentieth Century West* (Lawrence: University Press of Kansas, 1998).

Kris Fresonke and Mark Spence, eds., *Lewis and Clark Legacies:*

Memories and New Perspectives (Berkeley: University of California Press, 2004).

George Venn, "Soldier to Advocate: C.E.S. Wood's 1877 Diary of Alaska and the Nez Perce Conflict," *Oregon Historical Quarterly* 106 (Spring 2005): 34-75.

Most of my citations from the journals are drawn from *The Journals of Lewis and Clark*, abridged by Anthony Brandt (Washington, D.C.: National Geographic Adventure Classics, 2002).

Index

Absentee Shawnee Tribe, 152

Adams, Arlene, 46

Advertising, 32, 165: and environmentalism, 77-9, 91, 110, 167; Indians in, 26-7, 46-7, 110-11, 166-9

Advertising Council, 46, 77-9, 91, 165-6, 169

African Americans, 36, 127, 157-8

Allen, Barbara, 25

Allen, John Logan, 6, 20, 28, 55, 130, 142

Alliance of Tribal Tourism Advocates, 54

Alliance for the Wild Rockies, 97

Ambrose, Stephen, 20, 36, 81, 124: environmentalism of, 20, 27, 76, 108

American Rivers, 6, 8, 26-7, 75-6, 79, 107-11

Anrushi, Peter Attila, 118

Anthan, George, 8

Archibald, Robert, 25, 31, 47, 72, 77, 79, 85, 165: profile of, 31-7

Arikara Indians, 14, 82, 110

Ariwhite, Rod, 48-9

Arthur, Bill, 89

Astoria, Ore., 128-9, 150: bicentennial events in, 58-9, 129-33

Baird, Brian, 58, 80, 126, 127

Baker, Frederick, 7

Baker, Gerard, 7, 10, 50, 55, 60: profile on, 10-15

Baker, Page, 12

Ballard Canal (Seattle), 87-8

Basch, Dick, 59

Baumgart, Betsy, 136

Bedard, Irene, 168

Beres, Lee Anne Tryon, 18

Bereuter, Doug, 81, 114-15

Bergren, Bob, 164-5

Bingham, Dyani, 137

Bitterroot Mountains, 54

Blackfeet Indians, 24, 137

Black Hills, S. Dak., 12, 26, 53

Blackwood, Clint, 28, 137

Bond, Christopher, 98

Borlaug, David, 84, 159-62

Botkin, Daniel, 25, 70, 72, 104, 105

Braveheart, LaDonna, 42

Bry, Jonathan, 163-4

Burns, Ken, 6, 19-20, 71-2, 124

Bush, George W., 40, 57, 75, 97, 108, 110, 141, 171

Bussard, Michelle, 7, 45

Camp Wood, Mo., 100

Cape Disappointment, 117, 148, 150

Canaday, Brian, 96, 99

Castle, Marietta, 125

Celilo Falls, 4, 111-13

Chapman, Scott, 72

Charbonneau, Jean Baptiste (Pompey), 48, 49, 160

Charbonneau, Toussaint, 48

Charlottesville, Va., 74

Chinook Indians, 40, 57-60, 119, 149

Circle of Conservation Advisors (COCA), 75, 79-80

Circle of State Advisors (COSA), 75

Circle of Tribal Advisors (COTA), 7, 32, 45-7, 49, 62, 65, 75, 168-70: pamphlet by, 151-4

Clark, William, 4-5, 32, 81, 90, 100, 115, 132, 137: and Indians, 49, 51, 55, 64; journal entries by, 64, 70, 73, 82-3, 102-3, 130, 145, 148, 162; as western icon, 6, 18, 20, 30, 72, 143; and York, 36, 156-7

Clatsop Indians, 58-9

Clinton, William Jefferson, 72-3, 74

Coboway, Chief, 59

Coffman, Jack, 8

Coleman, Sara, 161

Columbia Gorge, 75-6

Columbia River, 113, 117, 118, 148, 162: conservation of, 8, 97, 104, 110; Indian rights to, 111-12; salmon in, 102-4

Columbia River Intertribal Fisheries Commission, 103

Commemorations, 4-5, 19, 21, 23, 57: language of, 40-1. *See also* Confluence Project; exhibits; Signature Events

Confederated Tribes of Grand Ronde, 4

Confederated Tribes of the Umatilla Indians, 61-2, 76

Confluence Project, 112-13, 117-20, 132, 150

Conner, Roberta "Bobbie," 24, 25, 45, 50, 61; profile on, 61-6

Conservation. *See* environmentalism

Corps II (exhibit), 7, 11, 51, 60, 170

Craig, Larry, 49, 55-6, 81

Craig, Ron, 157

Crow Indians, 152

Dams, 14, 26, 98, 110: environmental impact of, 71, 96, 103, 105-6, 112, 164; removal of, 27, 75, 78, 97

Daschle, Tom, 44, 82, 108-9, 171

Dawson, Michelle, 81

Destination: The Pacific (Signature Event), 58

DeVoto, Bernard, 100, 130

Discovering the Rivers of Lewis and Clark (exhibit), 6

Dorgan, Byron L., 163

Duncan, Dayton, 12, 22-3, 84

Environmentalism, 6-8, 171: in ads, 77-9, 91, 110, 167; funding for, 79-81; and Indians, 9, 22, 56, 76-7; land stewardship, 25-7, 29, 72-9, 82, 84-5, 162-3; river systems, 8, 75-6, 82, 96-99, 103-4, 106-11, 114, 162-5; species protection, 22, 25, 71-8, 97-8, 103-4, 109-11, 163; and tourism, 9, 27, 73-4, 79, 88, 98, 101-2, 106, 108, 115, 126-7. *See also names of conservation groups*

Exhibits: river conservation, 6, 27, 29, 107, 110; traveling, 6-7, 11-12, 29, 32, 36, 46, 70, 110, 154-6, 158-9, 160-1

Fish and fishing: Indian rights to, 65, 97, 102-4, 112; species protection, 97-8, 109. *See also* salmon

Fisher, David, 114

Forrester, Steve, 130, 133

Fort Clatsop, 117, 130, 132, 148, 149, 150

Fort Mandan, 29, 160

Fort Peck Dam, 105-6, 135

Frazier, Ian, 12

Friends of the Columbia Gorge, 75-6

Friends of Lewis and Clark of Pacific County, 112

Friends of the Missouri River, 164

Friends of the Wild Swan, 97

Garrison Dam, 14-15, 106, 110, 163

Gates of the Mountains (Mont.), 133, 136

Gear, Daniel Red Elk, 23

Geery, Peter, 101-2

G+G Advertising, 168-9

Giago, Tim, 23, 42

Goering, Karen, 166

Gray, Gerald, Sr., 169

Great Falls, Mont., 135-6

Great River Greenway, 114

Gutkoski, Joe, 74

Half Moon, Otis, 12

Hall, Brian, 157

Harrison, Kathryn, 4

Heritage tourism, 8-9, 27-8, 101, 124-6, 129-30, 136, 138-9, 159-60, 171

Herseth, Stephanie, 44

Hewlett Foundation, 35, 46

Hidatsa Indians, 12-14, 48, 60, 82, 110-11

Hoeven, John, 27

Hohman, Kathryn, 72

Hudson, Charles, 103

Hudson, Marilyn, 60

Idaho, 55, 127: Signature Event in, 56

Idaho State Legislature, 56, 78

Indians: in ads, 26, 46-7, 110-11, 166-9; in art, 4, 151; art of, 41, 46, 51, 54, 153; artifacts of, 46, 63, 81, 155-6; bicentennial involvement of, 7, 11-14, 18-19, 23-4, 29, 40-60, 62, 64-6, 135, 137, 151-4, 170-1; bicentennial, criticism of, 7, 12, 13-14, 24-5, 42, 45, 47-8, 50-4, 58-60, 62, 65, 137; casinos, 4, 63-4, 170; and Corps, 7, 21-4, 42-4, 137, 141, 154-6; and environmentalism, 9, 21, 56, 76-7, 82, 110; federal recognition of, 40, 47, 49, 57-8; fishing rights of, 65, 97, 102-4, 112; land reclamation by, 48-50, 53, 65; powwows, 43, 152; on reservations, 10, 13, 41-3, 47, 51, 55, 137; and tourism, 7, 9, 41-4, 54, 151-4; trade with, 57-8; unemployment of, 41-2, 43. *See also names of tribes*

"In the Footsteps of Lewis and Clark" (environmental campaign), 8

Izaak Walton League, 109

Jacobsen, Jane, 112-13
Jefferson, Thomas, 21-2, 70, 96, 98, 130, 141, 144, 148, 171
Jefferson City, Mo., 4
Jenkins, Chip, 149, 150
Johnson, Gary, 57-8
Johnson, Tim, 44
Johnson, Tony, 58-9
Johnston, Paul, 109

Kansas, 126
Kemmis, Daniel, 22
Kenslow, Tiffany, 76
Kiesau, Mary, 77, 82, 87: profile of, 87-92
Kulongoski, Ted, 4-5
Kuralt, Charles, 27, 107

Lands Council of Spokane, 85, 104
Land stewardship. See environmentalism
Lake Owyhee, 163
Lake Sakakawea, 14-15
Lemhi Shoshone Indians, 48-9, 102
Lewis, Meriwether, 4-5, 86, 90, 96-7, 148, 154, 158: and Indians, 54, 85, 137, 142; journal entries by, 54, 73, 100, 102, 104-5, 133; as naturalist, 21-2, 70-1; as western icon, 18, 20, 30, 72, 143
Lewis and Clark Boat House and Nature Center (Mo.), 101
Lewis and Clark Caucus, 18, 80, 163
Lewis and Clark Centennial (1905-06), 21, 29, 34, 40
Lewis and Clark Expedition, 23, 41, 44, 80, 87, 96-7, 112, 134, 148, 150, 162: artifacts of, 37, 81, 154-5, 158; cultural significance of, 5-6, 9, 20, 30, 85; and Indians, 7, 14, 21-4, 42-4, 48-9, 52, 54, 57-8, 64, 85, 137, 141-2, 156; maps of, 14, 45; politics of, 21, 72; reenactments of, 52-3, 97, 101-2, 124-5; species, records on, 22, 25, 70-1, 78, 86. See also Lewis and Clark journals
Lewis and Clark Explorer Train, 129, 131-2
Lewis and Clark Fort Mandan Foundation, 160
Lewis and Clark Highway (Hwy 12), 83

Lewis and Clark journals: Columbia River in, 102, 105; and environmentalism, 4, 25, 70-3, 82-3, 104, 108; Indians in, 42, 54, 64, 142; Missouri River in, 100, 104-5, 133
Lewis and Clark: The Journey of the Corps of Discovery (film), 6
Lewis and Clark Mount Hood Wilderness Act, 82, 162
Lewis & Clark: The National Bicentennial Exhibition (exhibit), 155-6, 158
Lewis and Clark National Historical Park, 132, 148, 149-50
Lewis and Clark Trail, 7, 55, 84, 99, 115, 134, 136, 148-50, 165: historical marketing of, 8, 18, 28, 74, 97, 128, 150
Lewis and Clark Trail Heritage Foundation, 45, 75
Limerick, Patricia Nelson, 127, 138
Lin, Maya, 112-13, 116, 116-20, 132, 150
Lloyd-Davies, Paul, 125
Lochsa River, 83, 84
Locke, Gary, 110, 112, 119
Lolo Motorway, 83-5
Lolo Pass, 82-5
Long Beach Peninsula (Wash.), 132-3
Long Camp (Idaho), 55
Louisville, Ky., 79, 90, 126
Lower-Brule Sioux Reservation, 42-3

Macfarlane, Gary, 85
Mahlum, Dale, 137
Maker, Leonard, 51-2
Mandan-Hidatsa-Arikara Nation, 161
Mandan Indians, 12-14, 48, 60, 70, 82, 110-11, 161
Martin, Darrell, 24, 77
Martz, Judy, 73
McCall, Tom, 152
Meadows, Sammye, 64, 66, 152, 153-4
Meares, John, 148
Medina, Janet, 136
Minthorn, Antone, 112, 120
Missouri, 4, 51. See also St. Louis, Mo.
Missouri Breaks, 73, 100, 136
Missouri Historical Society, 32-7, 46, 154, 165
Missouri River, 124, 128: conservation of, 8, 26-8, 75, 82, 97-9, 106-11, 163-4; dams on, 96-7, 105-6, 109, 110-11; fishing on, 97-8, 109; navigation of, 70,

96-7, 99-101; tourism on, 27, 98-9, 101-2, 106, 109, 114-15, 133, 161. *See also* Missouri Breaks
Missouri River Commission, 106
Missouri-Yellowstone Confluence Interpretive Center, 161
Monacan Indians, 23, 60
Montana, 4, 125, 127, 165: bicentennial events in, 28, 128-9, 133-7, 164
Montana Tribal Tourism Alliance, 137
Monticello, Va., 19, 21, 23-5, 57, 65-6, 141
Moore, Bob, 21
Mossett, Amy, 11, 14, 24, 41, 45, 49, 52, 59
Moulton, Gary, 70, 142
Mudge, Cindi, 59

National Council of the Lewis & Clark Bicentennial: and environmentalism, 6, 75, 77, 79-81, 89, 90-1; funding of, 11, 32, 35, 46, 79-81; structural collapse of, 32, 165; tribal relations with, 7, 45, 49
National Park Service, 7, 81, 132: Lewis & Clark maps, 14, 45
National Wildlife Federation, 109
Nehalem Indians, 58-9
Nez Perce Historic Trail Park, 84
Nez Perce Indians, 54-6, 60, 83, 113, 117, 119-20
Nez Perce Reservation, 55
Nez Perce Trail, 55
Nicandri, David, 35, 76-7
Nimiipu. *See* Nez Perce Indians
North Dakota: economic decline of, 8; environmentalism in, 82, 163; reservations in, 10, 14; Signature Event in, 53; tourism in, 27-8, 125, 159-62
Norton, Gale, 66, 73-4

Oceti Sakowin (Seven Council Fires of the Sioux), 53
Oklahoma: Osage in, 51-2; Shawnee in, 50-1
Olson, Jeff, 51
Opdahl, Barbara, 29
Opdahl, Harlan, 29
Oregon, 4, 29, 58-9
Orloff, Chet, 44
Osage Indians, 51-2
Osborn, John, 26, 71, 74, 84-5, 104-5
Othmar, James, 167-9

Park, Timothy, 120
Penny, Sam, 24
Perry, Kris, 84
Peterson, Keith, 78
Pine Ridge, S.Dak., 42
Pinkham, Allen, 45, 54, 56
Pioske, Scott, 125
Plume, Alex White, 42, 52-3
Pompey. *See* Charbonneau, Jean Baptiste
Pompey's Pillar (Mont.), 137
Pope, Carl, 26, 74-5, 85, 106
Portland, Ore., 29, 40, 129, 131
"Protecting the Rivers of Lewis and Clark" (environmental project), 6
Pugh, Jeanne Kelley, 136

Redden, James, 97-9, 110
Rehberg, Denny, 73
Richards-Cook, Daphne, 42-4, 53-4, 60
Rivers. *See names of rivers*; environmentalism
Roach, Lorraine, 78
Ronda, James, 13, 20, 30, 140, 158, 170: profile of, 140-5
Rothman, Hal, 127
Russell, Nancy, 76

Sacagawea (Sakakawea), 4, 24, 40, 48-9, 78, 160, 166, 168
Sacajawea. *See* Sacagawea.
Sakakawea. *See* Sacagawea.
Salmon, 102, 130: protection of, 18, 25, 56, 71, 75, 77, 78, 97-8, 103-4, 110
Sayce, Jim, 58
Scott, Wilfred, 120
Scovell, Joe, 58
Shawa, Nabiel, 133
Shawnee Indians, 50-1, 152
Shawnee Nation United Remnant Band, 50-1
Shively, Paul, 74, 79, 91
Shoshone Indians, 48-9, 102
The Sierra Club, 8, 74-5, 78, 79, 81, 84, 163-4: exhibit, 26-7; Wild America project, 88-91
Signature Events, 76, 170: in Idaho, 56; in Kans., 126; in Ky., 79, 90; in Mo., 34, 49-51, 124; in Mont., 135-7; in N. Dak., 53, 161; in S.Dak., 53-4; in Wash., 58, 117

About the Author

David Sarasohn is Associate Editor of *The Oregonian* in Portland, and a national columnist for the Newhouse News Service. For 2002 and 1994, Sarasohn's columns won First Place awards in the "Best of the West" contest, covering 13 states. In 2002, the Society of Professional Journalists awarded him the Pulliam Fellowship for Editorial Writers, sending him out on the Lewis and Clark Trail.

Sarasohn taught American history at Reed College, California State University-Northridge, Portland State University, and UCLA, where he received his Ph.D. His previous book was *Party of Reform: Democrats in the Progressive Era*, published by the University Press of Mississippi in 1989.

He has written for the *New York Times*, the *Washington Post*, *Harper's*, the *New Republic*, *Utne Reader*, *The Nation*, and numerous other publications. He has appeared on the *Today* show and *The MacNeil-Lehrer Newshour*, and was a regular on Oregon Public Broadcasting's *Seven Days*.

He has never seen anything quite like the Lolo Pass.

Sioux Indians, 41-4, 52-4, 152
Smith, Bill, 56
Smith, Gordon, 163
Snake River, 8, 75, 78, 97, 103-4, 110, 113, 117, 119
Snider, Cliff, 57
Sortino, Peter, 114
South Dakota, 82: economic decline of, 8, 42-3; reservations in, 41-2; Signature Event in, 53
Souvenirs, 19-20, 170: coins, 80; Indian-made, 46, 153
Spence, Mark, 29
Station Camp, Wash., 149
St. Charles, Mo., 51, 100-1, 128: Signature Event in, 124
St. Louis, Mo., 31: bicentennial events in, 32-7, 51, 114
Stone, Betty, 106-7, 135

Tamástslikt Cultural Institute, 63
Tecumseh, Chief (Shawnee), 50
Tent of Many Voices (Corps II exhibit), 51, 57, 60
Teton, Randy'L He-dow, 48
Thom, Dark Rain, 45, 47, 50
Tourism, 4, 7, 170-1: advertising for, 47, 77-9, 168; and environmentalism, 9, 27, 73-5, 78, 88, 90, 98, 101-2, 106, 108, 115, 126-7, 163; Indian involvement in, 9, 41-4, 54, 151-4; in Montana, 125, 129, 133-7; in Oregon, 4-5, 128, 129-32, 150; in N. Dak., 27-9, 159-62; negative effects of, 127, 138; rise in, 28
Trabucco, Chester, 128

Umatilla Indians, 60, 61-5, 76, 119
United States Army Corps of Engineers, 96, 98, 106, 109, 111

United States Congress, 21, 82, 98, 107, 162-3
United States Department of the Interior, 81: treaties, 51, 54, 58, 65, 103-4, 120; tribal recognition, 40, 47, 49, 57-8
United States Forest Service, 76, 84, 85
United States Government: and bicentennial, 7, 18, 80-1; Indians, treatment of, 13-14, 40, 47, 49, 51, 53, 55, 106; lawsuits against, 97-8, 109. See also names of branches, departments

Walden, Greg, 163
Washington (state), 28, 132: Signature Event in, 58
Weippe Prairie (Idaho), 55
The West, 22, 25, 71: icons of, 18, 20-1, 144; redefinition of, 8, 20, 29, 86, 138, 142, 159, 170-1
Whiting, Dan, 49
Wild America: Protecting the Lands of Lewis and Clark (environmental project), 88-91
Wilgus, Carl, 78
Withers, W. Wayne, 33, 34
Wodder, Rebecca, 27, 75, 79, 80, 107-10
Wood, Charles Erskine Scott, 55
Wood, Karenne, 23, 25
Wu, David, 158
Wyden, Ron, 82, 162-3

Yeager, Nik, 125
Yeager, Teresa, 125
Yellowstone River, 27, 97, 128
York, 36, 78, 126-7, 156-8, 166
Young Man Afraid of His Horses, 53

Ziak, Rex, 132